Adventures in Learning

to Trust God

By

Joy Boese

Joy Boese
Proverbs 3:5-6

Copyright © 2005 by Joy Boese

ISBN 0-7414-2466-5

Scripture taken from the HOLY BIBLE: NEW INTERNATIONAL VERSION ®. Copyright © 1973, 1978, 1984 by the International Bible Society. Used by permission of Zondervan Bible Publishers.

Published by:

INFINITY
PUBLISHING.COM

1094 New DeHaven Street, Suite 100
West Conshohocken, PA 19428-2713
Info@buybooksontheweb.com
www.buybooksontheweb.com
Toll-free (877) BUY BOOK
Local Phone (610) 941-9999
Fax (610) 941-9959

Printed in the United States of America

Printed on Recycled Paper

Published March 2005

CONTENTS

Introduction

Although I have aspired to write children's stories when I retire, I had never intended to write a book—and certainly not my autobiography. I have been too busy living life to pause and record it. I have been keenly aware that this was God's assignment. He is the One who has given me inspiration and ability. What I have set in writing are the peaks and valleys as God has brought them to my mind. As I review my life, my heart wells up with thanksgiving to God for His faithfulness to me.

On my first home assignment I was preparing the messages for missionary speaking tour of C&MA churches. God gave me a favorite memory verse to use for the theme of one message. Proverbs 3:5-6: *Trust* in the LORD with *all* your heart and lean *not* on your own understanding; in *all* your ways acknowledge him, and *he* will make your paths straight [emphasis mine]. The message was a testimony in which I shared lessons of learning to trust God.

When I returned to America the second time I was impressed to use the same theme. It was not until my third home assignment that I caught on, *God is giving me Proverbs 3:5-6 as my life verse!* God wanted me to learn to trust Him in *every* area of my life. Sometimes I even had to relearn a lesson I had apparently forgotten.

I have seen how God took me, a shy and often sickly child, and healed me repeatedly. God called me at age 12 to be a missionary. My parents wondered if I would have the stamina to fulfill the role. Through God's enabling I have enjoyed 35 years of missionary ministry. Much of it stretched my comfort zone, but God proved to be my Enabler and my Sufficiency.

My thanks goes to my family for allowing me to share our stories and for their corrections and input. Dad not only allowed me to peruse his personal journal from the late

i

1940's when we lived in Siam, but he also consistently filed my letters for the last 30 years. The more than 1,000 letters "to Mother and Dad," a hodge-podge of childhood diaries, and the journals I've kept in adulthood have verified countless details that would have slipped from my present-day memory.

Thank you to Paul and Kirsten who reviewed and clarified the chapter on Usha and life in the temple monastery.

A big thank you to my sister, Faith Tieszen, for painstakingly correcting my American grammar gone astray. She made many helpful suggestions for choice of words and organization of material.

A *very* big thank you to my sister, Melody Kenny, who repeatedly spent hours patiently making computer corrections on the manuscript for her computer challenged sister! Without her help this book would have been a chore rather than a joy to write.

Thank you to the dedicated prayer partners of the past 50 years who have prayed for my parents, Harvey and Grace Boese and their children, Joy, Faith, Timothy, Carol and Melody. This is your story of what God did as you interceded for us and God's work in Thailand.

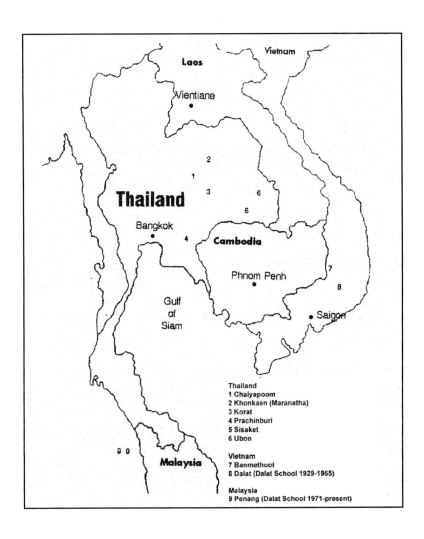

Laos

Vietnam

Vientiane
•

2

1
3   6
5

Thailand

Bangkok
•   4   **Cambodia**

Phnom Penh
•   7

8

Gulf
of
Siam   • Saigon

Thailand
1 Chaiyapoom
2 Khonkaen (Maranatha)
3 Korat
4 Prachinburi
5 Sisaket
6 Ubon

9 0
Malaysia   Vietnam
7 Banmethuot
8 Dalat (Dalat School 1929-1965)

Malaysia
9 Penang (Dalat School 1971-present)

iii

1—A Godly Heritage

"Help! Accident on board!" The radio operator frantically searched for a doctor. My family was aboard a freight ship, the *SS Steel Artisan*, traveling to Siam. It was August, 1952 and we were in the middle of the Pacific Ocean. Having sailed 11 days from San Francisco we were still 14 days away from Manila, Philippines. The nearest land was Guam, a good three days distance at top speed. There were four passenger cabins with three bunks each. Our family occupied one cabin with my younger sister, Faith and I sharing a bunk. At ages four and seven we were the only children on board.

A crew member doing maintenance work needed to put a metal stud into a cabin wall. Since it would be shot out of a gun the ship's passenger deck was cleared in case the stud should go through the wall to the outside. Faith and I were amusing ourselves pushing chairs around the deck. In our crepe soled shoes we pattered softly around unaware of any impending danger. Coming around a blind corner I found myself suddenly stunned and lying in a pool of blood. The stud had indeed come through the metal wall and struck my right thigh. It continued through and lodged in my left leg. My sudden cry brought crew and passengers alike racing to the scene on deck. Someone with first aid experience applied pressure to blood vessels to stop further hemorrhage.

The ship radio man's call for help was finally answered with, "Wait." It meant wait until the patient gets better or wait until he dies. In other words, the other ship was not coming. Insistently our officer radioed again, "It's a child." Both ships then changed course to meet as quickly as possible.

While waiting for the rendezvous a crew member heard Dad whistling. "How can the child's father sing in a time like this?" he asked another missionary passenger.

"Do you know what he is whistling?" she asked. "It's 'The Love of God.'"

1

In God's providence there was an American doctor vacationing on a Japanese weather boat in the area. Within a couple hours the doctor had boarded our ship and surgically removed the stud from my left leg. There was pale yellow matter around the screw end of the stud. Because this was assumed to be bone tissue, it was thought that both femur bones had been penetrated. The doctor forbid me to walk or do any weight bearing until x-rays could be taken whenever we reached land.

My childish concerns had been focused on the physical unpleasantries. I complained about the itchy wool army blanket I was carried on from the first aid room to the cabin. I cried that my favorite little yellow sunsuit was thrown away into the ocean when it was bloody and torn from the stud whizzing through it. The daily penicillin shots probably hurt me no more than they did the tender-hearted first mate who had to administer them.

Two weeks later when the ship arrived in Manila, Philippines an ambulance met the ship and took us right to the hospital for x-rays. A retired American army doctor read the films and shook his head in disbelief. "I've been a doctor through two wars and seen many strange things. But this stud went into the right leg, around the large femur bone, into the left leg and around the bone again. You must have a God." Everyone knew it was truly a miracle that no bones had been broken. Mother said to me, "Joy, God has spared your life for a reason."

My parents came from farming families. Mother was the seventh of ten children born to Richard and Mary Chadderdon in Minnesota in 1921. Dad was born in 1917, the only child to Henry and Susie Boese. He grew up in a Mennonite community in South Dakota. Both my parents were called to full time Christian service and met in St. Paul Bible College. They married in June, 1944. With World War II still in progress they accepted an assignment to pastor the Christian and Missionary Alliance (C&MA) church in the small coal mining town of Hiawatha, Utah. Early on Mother's Day, May 13, 1945, I was born Joyce Susan Boese in Price, Utah. Grandma Susie Boese was one of the few who have called me "Joyce" even though I was really intended to be "Joy."

It was later in life that I learned of my godly heritage. Both sets of my paternal great grandparents had been Mennonites of German descent who immigrated from Ukraine to America seeking religious freedom in late 1874. They settled in South Dakota. Grandpa Henry Boese was the eldest of 11 children.

Grandma Susie (Schmidt) Boese, was the 13th sibling among 16 (including one adopted brother). Grandma's mother, Aganetha Voth Schmidt, died when Susie was five years old. Her mother was a prayer warrior who dedicated her children to God and interceded much for them. Seven of Grandma's siblings became missionaries in China and three others were ministers. By 1953 it was calculated that this family had served a total of 914 years in full time Christian service. Her nephew, Paul Bartel, of China and Hong Kong served under the C&MA until his death in 2001. He was almost 97 years old.

Although Grandma Boese was not one of those who served overseas, she, like her mother, prayed faithfully for God's servants. It is no wonder that her son and daughter-in-law, Harvey and Grace Boese should serve God in Thailand and the homeland for over 50 years. Three grandchildren became missionaries, another a pastor's wife and the youngest took up the gauntlet of prayer.

In 1946 my parents received word from the C&MA Foreign Missions Department that they were assigned as missionaries to East Siam. Excitedly they pored over a map to see where God was taking them. Never having seen a picture of Siam, they wondered what kind of a house or hut they would live in. It was not easy for my Boese grandparents now living in southern California to say goodbye to their only child and only grandchild. They knew it would be five years before we were to return to the homeland.

We joined a group of returning missionaries on the *SS Marine Adder*, a freighter that had been used as a troop ship during the war. My parents were the first new C&MA missionaries to go to Siam after the war. Essentially the whole mission team traveled together. On December 23, 1946 we sailed out of Oakland, California. By the third day a winter storm was tossing our vessel severely. Dad noted in his journal that all our meals were taken standing up—the tablecloths were wetted down and chairs tied in a corner. Two and a half weeks later our ship docked in Hong Kong where all the missionaries were given smallpox vaccinations before boarding another steamer, the *Golden West*.

We continued to the Gulf of Siam, arriving in Bangkok January 24, 1947. My parents and I (now 20 months old) were among those assigned to stay in the Oriental Hotel, a modest ordinary accommodation. It was furnished with hospital beds confiscated from Bangkok Christian Hospital by the Japanese invaders during the war. Chickens wandered around in the halls and mosquito nets graced the bedposts. [Today the Oriental has become a top-rated hotel in Asia.]

Bangkok was a quiet unassuming city on the banks of the Chao Phraya River. It was crisscrossed by so many canals that it was known as the Venice of the East. Rice, charcoal and coconuts were brought into the city by slow moving river barges. Hundreds of small boats plied the waterways with colorful fresh produce creating literal floating markets. At daybreak Buddhist laymen could be seen paddling canoes for saffron robed monks as they paused at each home or pier to receive the daily alms. The postman's delivery route was more than likely demarcated by canals than roads.

In the late 1940's paved roads were still few in number. Bicycles and passenger *samlaws* (Thai word for three wheeler) pedaled more or less on the left side of the road, a British influence. Noisily clanging electric street cars had right of way on the main streets. They provided a choice of first class seats with a firm kapok cushion or hard wooden second class seats at half price. Well worn wooden buses, poorly maintained unpainted trucks and a few old cars vied for whatever space was left on the road. As the capital of Siam, Bangkok was therefore the seat of the government. Although the ninth king of the Chakri dynasty was reigning, political decisions were made by the prime minister and parliament. The country had become a constitutional monarchy in 1932. Siam was still recovering from the effects of a world war so the economy was struggling. This was the scene the missionaries encountered as they arrived early in 1947.

After 12 days all the formalities of customs and inspections and immigrations were completed. Then our Boese family joined the Theo Ziemers, Bob Chrismans, Asher Cases and John Perkins families on a wood-burning steam engine train at 6 a.m. for the 13 hour trip north. By 8 p.m. we arrived in Korat for an overnight stay in a local hotel. We were sticky hot, tired and covered with flecks of black soot. Mother asked for some warm

4

water to give me a bath and the bell boy brought her tea! The following day we re-boarded the train for another soot dusted seven hour ride to Khonkaen, Siam—our destination. It was February 6, 1947 nearly seven weeks since leaving Upland, California, USA.

Khonkaen was a sleepy town of single and double story shop houses that lined rough dirt roads. The homes were built on stilt-like posts. A large earthen water jar was usually strategically set beside the wooden ladder or stairs up to the porch. This facilitated the custom of removing one's shoes downstairs and pouring a dipper or two of tepid water over one's dusty feet before ascending barefoot into the house.

Although homes lacked mosquito screens, metal rods a finger's width in diameter barred intruders from every window. Coconut, banana and papaya trees were most commonly growing nearby. A simple dome shaped bamboo coop was home to a few family chickens. A skinny mongrel dog often hung around for any scraps of food that might be salvaged. At nightfall the town twinkled with single yellow lights of kerosene lanterns in each home for a couple short hours.

The sleepy hush of the night was broken about 4:00 a.m. when the roosters crowed the dawn of a new day. The familiar acrid odor of smoking wood chips igniting charcoal in clay fire pots was accompanied by the soft whir of woven bamboo hand fans energetically coaxing the black coal chunks into flame. Women put their rice pots on to cook and then hurried to the open air fresh market for the day's supply of meat, fruit and vegetables. By 5:30 a.m. all the better hunks of meat and produce would be gone. It was into this lifestyle that the missionaries of the post war era adjusted their lives.

Initially we shared a house with another missionary family. It was clapboard single walls and we used cardboard to fill cracks where the boards were warped. Dad noted in his journal that it took five days for a mattress maker to complete his work for us while Dad made a wooden bedstead. But it was not until one year after arriving in the tropics that we got our first kerosene refrigerator.

My parents began Siamese language study with a government school teacher who came before and after school hours (6:30

5

- 7:30 a.m. and 5:00 - 6:00 p.m.). They studied the language eight hours a day, five days a week, while I was cared for by a Siamese Buddhist baby sitter and picked up the language naturally.

The following year I had my first plane ride, going to French Indochina for the annual mission conference. It was held in Dalat, the highland resort town where the missionary kids' (MK) school had been founded in 1929 by Miss Armia Heikkinen. At the conference my parents were assigned to Ubon. We moved there in June and my parents continued language study for a second year. At three years of age I now spoke the local language effortlessly. I often enjoyed playing "language teacher" with my parents on the spacious front porch of our Thai house.

My sister, Faith Marie Boese was born in September. She was only four months old when we took her on her first village trip. In those early years we had no vehicle so Dad hired a couple oxcart drivers to transport us into villages for 10-14 day preaching trips. Mother somehow balanced baby Faith, toddler Joy, a water jug and an umbrella between the huge wheels of one oxcart. The mattresses, mosquito nets, canned goods, lantern, camp stove and literature were packed on a second oxcart. I can still picture Dad in his pith helmet and khaki shorts walking ahead of the oxcarts through the dry rice paddy fields. Arriving in a village we would approach the headman and we would be invited to sleep on the porch of his house. The sight of a foreign family always drew a crowd. Our every action was watched by dozens of pairs of curious eyes. We modestly bathed wearing the native wrap-around skirts at the public well or in the river just like the villagers, but we were never without an audience. As kids we always felt we were on display. We resented having our chins affectionately pinched by curious villagers, or being peeked at under the mosquito net at night.

At the mission conference in Bangkok the next year my parents were delighted to be assigned to a pioneer ministry in a new province, Prachinburi. It was months before a house was finished in the town for us. Dad rented a storefront near the railroad station for gospel services. When he played his trombone, the people gathered to see what we did. Mother taught the children songs and Bible stories illustrated with a colorful poster-sized picture roll.

6

It was the evening of September 15, 1950 and we were having family devotions after supper as was our custom. I began to cry as Mother finished reading the story of Adam and Eve in the Garden of Eden. "What's the matter, Joy?" my parents queried.

"I don't want to go to hell," I sobbed. The Holy Spirit had brought conviction to my heart. Once in a children's meeting I had spoiled Mother's object lesson on believing and trusting God. She had invited any child who believed her to come and get a coin which she claimed was inside the match box. When one brave child ventured forward Mother opened the box. She was horrified to discover it was empty! I was the guilty party who had taken the coin. My first concern after praying for salvation was my sister. Faith was not yet two years old and I was afraid *she* would go to hell since she hadn't prayed for salvation.

One incident that remains clearly in my mind was when I was five years old. Our family was vacationing at a beach on the Gulf of Siam. It was like camping in a rented bungalow. The evening meal was usually with a mosquito net over the table to keep sand flies, gnats, and mosquitoes off us while we ate. Missionaries Paul and Priscilla Johnson and family, our best friends, were in the bungalow next to us. Bryan was my age. Both of us had left America as toddlers and had no memory of our grandparents. (Black and white photos of relatives were the only tangible evidence of a world outside our Siam.)

One day we formed a plan. Early the next morning I convinced Mother to make a lunch for Bryan and me. It was candy, crackers and jelly. I hurried over to Johnsons' bungalow only to find Bryan still sleeping under his mosquito net. I had to wait for him to eat his breakfast oatmeal and then we started off hand in hand down the sandy beach. We were headed for a fishing village several miles away. After about 20 minutes we sat under a clump of bamboo trees to have our lunch. When Bryan boyishly smeared the candy wrapper on my face, I got mad at him and we turned around. Our intention had been to get a boat to go to America to see our grandparents who lived "on the other side of the ocean." We told our parents we couldn't find a boat. That was the nearest I ever came to running away from home!

The following year, 1952, Bryan's parents were shot by bandits in a Thai village in Udorn province. Bryan was away at

Dalat School in first grade and I was in school in California where we were on furlough. The three Johnson children were instantly orphaned and returned to America to live with their maternal grandparents. The shock and sorrow of this tragedy was forever implanted on our family. Thereafter there were no toy guns in the Boese household.

By mid 1951 we boarded a ship to America for our first furlough. We lived with Grandma and Grandpa Boese in southern California. America seemed so strange to us kids. I recall that Faith and I would shyly stand in a corner of a church and talk Siamese together. As a first grader I loved walking to school and the smell of pepper trees along the sidewalk. Golden California poppies grew profusely in the vacant field across the street from our house. In the classroom at noon I loved the raisins and other special treats Mother put in my school lunch box.

On the mission field we had known rather sparse Christmases due to the lack of toys to buy in Siam. My parents were pleased to think that this year they could delight their little girls with American playthings. But to their surprise my entire wish list consisted of only two items—a shiny red purse and a Bible. Of course I received both and more than that. The Bible was highly prized as I was just learning to read.

Before our furlough ended we drove as a family to the annual council of The Christian and Missionary Alliance in Atlanta, Georgia in mid 1952. Then we traveled back to California by way of Minnesota and had a family reunion with Mother's relatives in June. It was the last time I saw my Grandpa Chadderdon who died while we were on shipboard returning to Siam; the telegram telling us of Grandpa's death never reached us. Weeks later when a letter came telling of a funeral Mother realized that it was her father's funeral. It was on this return trip to Siam, which was now called Thailand, that I was accidentally shot, and God preserved my life to serve Him.

For my parents' second term of service we returned to live in Prachinburi province to the same little sun-parched town with a sprinkling of scrawny trees in east Thailand. It was far from the coast and there was no breeze to give relief from the year-round heat. During the rainy season the tiled roofs and galvanized tin eaves troughs directed the precious water through down spouts into large earthen jars. Torrential rains made mud holes of the narrow dirt lanes serving the town. Bicycles, three wheeled *samlaws* and oxcarts made up the sparse traffic. An occasional poorly maintained wooden bus would rumble and jerk uncertainly through to the next town. A wood burning steam engine train ran daily between the capital, Bangkok, and the Cambodian border, pausing at the dull brown and cream colored railway station for passengers, mail and freight.

By this time our family had acquired a very important commodity—an army surplus jeep. It made ministry in the villages much more accessible and was a time saver compared to the oxcarts and broken down buses we had used previously.

Two months after returning to the field Mother was due to deliver another sibling. Our little town had no hospital, doctor or nurse—only a Thai military medic. A hospital where she could have the baby was probably six hours or more away.

Dad was out on a village trip the day when Mother went into early labor. She asked Faith (four years old) and me (seven) to be extra good because she was in labor pain. Being the big sister and thinking how I could help, I went into the kitchen and returned to Mother carrying a butcher knife.

"Just tell me when, Mommy," I innocently offered. I knew the baby was inside Mother's abdomen so would obviously need help getting out. (My aspirations to be a midwife began early!)

Late that evening when Dad returned from the village he realized we would not be able to wait until morning to get to the hospital. He persuaded the local medic to come with us in case the baby was born en route. The medic was in the front seat beside

Dad. Mother, Faith and I curled up as best we could in the back seat and started out for the midnight trip to Bangkok. After bumping over rough gravel roads for about 125 miles we finally arrived at the Adventist Hospital as the sun rose over the city. We were just in time as Timothy Richard Boese was born shortly after Mother got into the hospital. Faith and I were embarrassed to be in the back of the Jeep in our pajamas in broad daylight. It offended our sense of modesty. But we were delighted to welcome our new brother.

In January 1953 I was the little blonde girl among 11 older MK's with a home permanent who boarded an Air Vietnam propeller plane in Bangkok. I was proud to be a *big* girl going off to school with my older peers. It was the custom that parents ease the pain of parting by preparing small "going away" gifts to be opened on the plane by their children. Wondering what surprise I would have I could hardly wait to unwrap my gift. Would it be a special sweet or something to wear or an item to use? In later years the excitement was tempered by tears—seeing our parents sadly waving goodbye for our three and a half month absence as well as our own longings to be in our parents' warm embrace. The anticipation of being with peers usually won out over the sad emotions.

After a hot and sticky hour's layover in Phnom Penh, Cambodia for refueling we re-boarded for our next stop of Saigon, French Indochina. In the Saigon Guest Home during that first night away from our parents, most of us had a cry or two of homesickness. The city was hot and humid making sleep very uncomfortable. We got some relief by getting up several times in the night to take a cold shower. The next morning we eagerly took another plane up to Dalat, our mission boarding school for Southeast Asia. This was to be our home for two semesters a year.

Arriving in Dalat it seemed to me that we had touched down in a forest of pine trees with one small hut on a hill for a terminal. The cool air of the mountain highland resort was a refreshing change from the tropical plains we had just left. I was glad to reach into my overnight bag and don a sweater Mother had thoughtfully tucked in. As the school car came up the hill to the boarding school grounds—there it was: "Villa Alliance" on the gate posts. It was the address I would write on all my letters until I graduated from high school some ten years later.

The school boasted two main buildings. The two story French style concrete structure at the top of the hill housed the girls' dorm upstairs where the school nurse, Lois Chandler doubled as house mother. Downstairs was the dining room and office. In the single story behind was a kitchen where the Vietnamese cooks prepared three regular meals a day for about 25 students and staff. Attached to that was what we referred to as "outback" where the laundry was washed and ironed. A fire was kept burning under a huge square water tank. This was the source of hot water for our twice a week baths. A mountain tribesman was hired to carry pails of hot water up the stairs to the bathrooms. It was one pail per tub per student.

The second building was a single story to the right of the main building. The auditorium and boys' dorm occupied the whole floor. It was also living accommodations for Harold and Agnes Dutton and their preschooler, Teddy who were the boys' dorm parents. Because it was built on the side of the mountain there was a large concrete basement and two classrooms below. Miss Armia Heikkinen taught the 12 students in grades one through six in the first room. Miss Ruth Chamberlain taught the remaining ten or so junior high and high school kids in the adjacent room. In the first grade that semester there was one boy. Next to him in grade two were—my roommates, Betty Ruth Clingen and Marilyn Graven and me.

I knew Marilyn previously as our families had met at the Thai-Cambodian border for a picnic when we were pre-schoolers. It didn't take long to get acquainted with Betty Ruth who was an MK from Laos. Our dorm parents read bedtime stories and prayed with us at night. In the mornings they assigned us "big sisters" from the upper grades to have devotions with us.

Our big sisters made sure we were up and dressed in time for breakfast. They checked that we had properly cleaned our room before going off to our classes. They also helped us with our letters home and gave advice. We appreciated the sibling warmth they extended and the model they set for us. In later years we in turn would become the big sisters.

Everything was new and interesting to me as a shy second grader. We played Capture the Flag on Jacksons' Hill, softball at the old airport field and had pine cone fights on campus. Fridays were always "late nights" for which a special activity was planned. We looked forward with happy anticipation to a taffy pull, games or roller skating in the big school basement.

One of the boarding school traditions was that every Sunday afternoon after rest time we wrote a letter home. Likewise, my mother faithfully wrote to us children every week, (and has continued to do so for 50 years). I always looked forward to not only the letters, but also the postage stamps on the envelopes. Most of the MK's were stamp collectors, so mail time was a double joy. In later years Dad began writing to us also, alternating weeks with Mother. Our family ties were strongly bound together through these regular letters.

Within the first semester at Dalat I had difficulty keeping up with my peers and tired easily. The nurse thought that Dalat's mountain altitude was a problem for me. She took me to the local French doctor. His diagnosis was that I had an arrhythmia, an irregular heartbeat that tired me. I was given orders for physical limitations—not to run or engage in strenuous activity. Upon receiving this news, far away in Thailand my parents prayed for healing and wrote letters to their prayer warriors. Within about a year God answered their prayers and healed my heart enabling me to engage in full activities. I could run and play with my friends once again.

Travel back and forth from Bangkok to Dalat School every semester was pretty routine and predictable to us MK's. There were the familiar immigration forms to fill in with passport information for each of us. Usually the oldest child in our group would be responsible to carry all the passports and fill in the forms. At times this was a rather weighty job when the eldest student among us was only 12 years old. As a young teenager it was my job on more than one occasion. Like my predecessors I prided myself in taking this "grown up" position. We felt honored to be trusted rather than feeling put upon.

It was probably April, 1954 when I was nearly nine years old that I experienced fear and uncertainty in our travels. Civil war had erupted quite suddenly in the Chinese section of Saigon. Poor and slow communication systems of that era did not enable word to reach Dalat School before we Thailand MK's flew out of Dalat's airport. As we deplaned in Saigon about an hour later we wondered about the columns of smoke billowing up in the distance over the city. Harold Dutton who met us at the airport was now the manager of the Saigon Guest Home. He told us part of the city was burning and there was fighting going on. He abruptly whisked us from the airport to the empty home of vacationing missionaries. He said he would come back to us as soon as he could and the Vietnamese servants would fix us something to eat in the meantime. Then he determinedly set off across the town to rescue his wife and two preschoolers who were crouched under a bed at the Guest Home in an effort to dodge any stray bullets.

Naturally we were sobered and frightened at the news. It was further unnerving to us to hear and see the army tanks refueling at the depot right next to the home where we had been deposited. Although we could play outside in the yard, the sight of tanks rumbling back and forth before our eyes was too disquieting to do so. In addition to this we did not speak Vietnamese and could not communicate with anyone. By nightfall the Duttons were back and we all felt safe again. During that time, Bonnie Kerr, an MK two years older than I modeled spiritual maturity as a big sister and shared Psalm 91 with me. Thus I experienced the very real comfort of God's Word at a young age. The next day we were on our way to Bangkok as scheduled.

On occasion Asia's antiquated telegraph systems failed to deliver the news of our flight arrival data to the office. As a result there would be no one to meet us at the airport. One time it was in Saigon where the dozen of us MK's wandered around waiting to be picked up. The airport personnel didn't understand English, and of course we couldn't speak Vietnamese or French. About closing time an airline official contacted a missionary friend, Mr. D.I. Jeffrey, saying there were some American kids waiting there at the airport. No one had come for them. When the missionary came to investigate he found us and hustled us into taxis. We were taken to the Saigon Guest Home where they had never received the telegram saying we were coming.

Another time our parents were impatiently waiting in the Bangkok Guest Home to hear when we would be arriving—and again the telegram went astray. It was anticlimactic for us to arrive "home" in Bangkok and not see the familiar faces of our parents waiting for us. However, it was our turf and we could speak Thai so someone phoned the Guest Home to announce our arrival. In

13

less than an hour we were all enjoying the warm hugs of our parents and soon forgot the momentary disappointment. It was good to be home again.

During the French Indochina War it was reported that Viet Minh troops would be advancing towards the little town of Dalat nestled in the wooded mountains. Although the school term was due to end in only a week or so, the American military sent a plane to evacuate us. The high school students took exams early. We "little kids" had to take care of ourselves and pack our own suitcases. I felt very grown up packing my bag. The unexpectedly early trip home obliterated any feelings of danger for us younger ones. However our parents were very concerned for our safety. We kids simply chalked up the experience as something exciting to talk about.

When I was ten years old and Faith was seven, my parents decided that we would not return to Dalat for the next semester. I needed to be under a doctor's care in Bangkok, for some ongoing health problems. Since our home was in Prachinburi at the time, arrangements were made for us to board with missionaries, the Asher Cases, and attend the International School in Bangkok. Everyday we had to pick our way through a sidewalk open air morning market, walk past an ornate Hindu temple and climb on a street car for the ride to school. Our classmates were the children of ambassadors and embassy workers. I don't recall any Christians among the students or staff. We were glad that one semester was all that was necessary there. We wanted to get back to boarding school, where we felt secure with Christian teachers and familiar MK friends.

After nearly four years in Prachinburi province Dad was elected chairman of the Thailand missionaries. That meant we had to move to the headquarters in Korat, a growing city in the center of northeastern Thailand. It was considerably different from living in the small town where we were previously. Korat city was home to the mission secretary and bookkeeper. Missionaries engaged in radio programming, city church ministries and village evangelism lived there as well as some new missionaries in Thai language study. We suddenly had missionary coworkers to fellowship with and other MK's to play with during school vacation. There were several markets and big stores to shop in. The streets were paved and the traffic included cars and trucks of every description. Trains passed through day and night.

Within a couple months of getting settled in Korat a fourth sibling was born into our family. Carol Ruth Boese was happily welcomed by Faith, Tim and me. It was fun to have a baby in the house again.

Meanwhile, God was continuing to work in my life. At age 12 in the dormitory at Dalat School I arrived at another milestone in my life. As I lay on my bed that night, the day's events played back in my mind. Then I found myself thinking of millions of people who were dying and going to hell without Christ. Suddenly I realized that I was to be a missionary. There was no thunderbolt from heaven nor any scripture verse blazing out at me. It was just a deep seated knowledge that I was to be a missionary. It was as certain to me as my salvation. It was my call to be a missionary. For as long as I could remember I had wanted to be a nurse. But when God called me to be a missionary I simply said, "Okay, God, I'll be a missionary." I gave up my desire to be a nurse. I never thought to tell anyone about it until two or three years later when my mother happened to ask me what I wanted to be when I grew up.

In 1958 at the end of my parents' second term on the mission field, we returned to America by way of Europe. My parents had realized that I would finish high school before their next five year term was over, so they decided we would take the trip of our lifetime. My sister, Faith and I flew from school in Vietnam to Singapore at the end of April to meet my parents. There we boarded a Dutch passenger ship the *Willem Ruys*. It was the ship carrying the last of the Dutch refugees out of Indonesia. I was allowed to eat in the adult dining room with my parents. But my three siblings had to eat in the kids' dining room for the under-twelves. As a family we didn't like this separation at meal time but we kids did enjoy the early morning tea served in the cabin—particularly the cookies and sugar cubes.

Our first stop was in Ceylon (now Sri Lanka) and then we went on through the Suez Canal where the merchants in their little boats came out to our ship to sell their wares. I was especially impressed to find that the sun, a fiery red ball was just setting at 10 o'clock at night. Our stop in Naples, Italy was memorable to me for our sight-seeing to the catacombs. I was also pleased that my parents bought me a pretty red accordion in Italy for only 60 dollars. Our ship passed by the Rock of Gibraltar and finally docked in Rotterdam, Holland, where we disembarked.

Although it was already May it felt like winter to us after six years in the tropics. The Alliance home and headquarters, Parousia, was in Wassenaar where the Konemann family welcomed us. I celebrated my 13th birthday there with tulips, an ice cream cake and a Dutchman doll. The four of us kids embarrassed my parents by our ravenous thirst for milk. The fresh milk tasted so good to us after the years of foamy powdered milk on the mission field! I especially loved the special Dutch chocolate sprinkles on my bread at breakfast.

A visit to Holland in miniature, Madurodam, was another favorite memory. On Pentecost Day a missions rally was held, and Dad and Elze Stringer were the missionary speakers for the occasion. Then we took a modern international train to Switzerland. We kids loved the down comforters we slept under in the home where we stayed by the Lake of Thun. The giant pansies and a countryside prettier than the popular tourist photos etched themselves indelibly on my mind. Then we rode the train back to Belgium where we stayed with the Knecht family and toured the World's Fair. But all that travel was pretty tough on two year old Carol and Mother who was pregnant with another child.

A ferry took us across the Straits of Dover to spend a week in London. We stayed in Bowling Green at the Overseas Missionary Fellowship home. Due to a bus strike we ended up doing a lot of walking or taking the subway. We managed to see early manuscripts of the Bible at the British Museum, St. James Park and the changing of the guard at Buckingham Palace. A train then took us to South Hampton where we boarded another passenger ship to New York City.

The Statue of Liberty was our first glimpse of America since 1952—six years before. I felt more like a tourist coming to America than a native citizen returning home. When we arrived ashore we found that missionary colleagues, the Webbers, were due to return to Thailand. They had been given a big brown 1947 Chrysler to use during furlough and they passed it on to us.

That weekend we drove up to Toronto, Canada to meet people at the Avenue Road Alliance Church. These people had supported us for many years even though we had never met them. Since our family of six was too large to be entertained in one home, we were divided among three homes. Women wore hats to church in 1958, but our missionary family was quite obvious--we were hatless! I tried to act grown up, but felt a bit self conscious and out of place.

Continuing across the United States we visited as many friends and relatives as possible. This included a big Chadderdon family reunion in Minnesota at the County Fair Grounds. I was a bit overwhelmed to meet all these relatives at once. In fact, I felt closer to my MK friends than to these cousins, aunts and uncles that I hardly knew.

By July 4, Grandpa Boese's 74th birthday, we arrived in California. We moved into a house that Grandma and Grandpa had bought just one block from the elementary school. We did not know it then, but this house would become our family home in America for the next 40 years. After every four or five year term on the mission field we would come back to this house for our year's furlough.

It was a very stressful year for me as an American junior high kid. Dad was often away on speaking tours. At home Mother was sick in bed most of the time with her fifth pregnancy. It meant that I got breakfast and made lunches for my siblings. I also worked in the school snack bar at noon and earned a free lunch. On weekends I cleaned the house and did the family laundry.

Then Dad was called home from a trip when Mother went into early labor. Melody Dawn Boese was born one month premature. Even though she weighed less than five pounds the doctor allowed her to come home from the hospital in a couple of days. Should there be an emergency, the hospital was only five minutes' drive away. The doctor also knew that missionary salaries were rather limited. At 13 I was delighted to have a baby in the house. The first three nights Melody was home I ran down the stairs at her slightest whimper for the privilege of carrying her from her crib to Mother's bed. I soon became the built-in baby sitter.

Spiritually, I was growing. Youth rallies and church activities prompted me to witness to classmates. I remember only one friend who accepted my invitation to attend a rally. It was to hear Dr. Richard Harvey who preached powerfully on hell. One evening, the pastor at our C&MA church in Pomona preached on the Holy Spirit. It was the first time I remembered hearing such a message. I responded to the altar call that night to invite the Holy Spirit to come into my life by faith.

Finishing the eighth grade in a California school was a big occasion which culminated with a graduation ceremony. I was excited to be wearing my first pair of high heeled shoes and a new store bought pink dress with white lace trim. My first grade teacher from Upland Elementary School joined my mother and three siblings to attend the special event. My dad and my grandparents were busy at home packing up the last of our belongings to return to Thailand. Returning home from graduation that night I changed into a pair of jeans. By midnight we had the brown Chrysler packed to capacity including the rack on the roof. Baby Melody, Faith and I squeezed into what was left of the back seat, while my parents with Tim and Carol were in the front. For a third time Grandma and Grandpa were saying goodbye to their only child and all five of their grandchildren as we left for another five year term in Thailand. It is no wonder we felt God's blessing on our family so many times. Grandpa and Grandma gave their all to Jesus, without reserve.

Driving all night from southern California to Oakland as a sardine family in an 11 year old brown Chrysler we must have looked a sight as we pulled into the Home of Peace about noontime. The Home was a simple nondenominational guest house for missionary travelers arriving or departing from the West Coast. In less than 24 hours I had gone from the excitement of eighth grade graduation to the emotional upheaval of saying farewells to grandparents I had grown to love. I was thankful to stretch out into a nice clean bed after the cramped night in the car. However, I was disappointed there really was not time to explore the Home and the spacious yard as the next day we had to drive down to the harbor and board our ship.

The freighter we boarded had a total passenger list of two missionary families: Harvey and Grace Boese with their five children and Bill and Minnie Miess with three children. Miesses' oldest son, Sam was staying in America for high school. Their daughter Miriam was a year younger than I. Tom and Sally were about the same ages as my sister, Faith and brother, Tim. Because of crossing the international dateline we missed a Sunday. So we held church on Monday instead. Miriam and I played our accordions for the worship service. Since the three or four week ocean trip made us kids six weeks late for school in Dalat that meant that as a ninth grader I would have to do make up homework during Christmas vacation. It was not a pleasant thought.

High school at Dalat was academically competitive and full of social peer pressure. Many new teachers had been added to the staff and each one enriched my life. One of the dorm parents introduced me to the writings of A.W. Tozer. His books fed my great spiritual hunger. I often read my Bible by flashlight under the blankets so as not to disturb my three roommates, or I would have my personal devotions in the hall or bathroom an hour before the rising bell. Guest speakers during spiritual emphasis weeks stirred my soul and I was thirsting for more of God. On vacation at home I perused Dad's library for books on prayer. Dad's example of rising early to be alone with God contributed to my desires for intimacy with God.

One memorable Sunday evening in a youth meeting at the school a film on Africa was shown. The youth sponsor said that he was trusting God to use the film to speak to us teenagers about being missionaries. I smugly thought to myself *God won't call me because He already called me. He doesn't need to tell me twice.* However, it was through that film that God showed me that nursing was to be a part of my missionary ministry! What I had given up as a 12 year old—my desire to be a nurse—was now being given back to me. I learned that God truly does give us the desires of our hearts.

At home between school semesters we lived in Ubon, where my parents had completed their second year of language study. It was where we had traveled by oxcarts to the villages. This time we had a Land Rover for transportation. Mother and Dad had been among the dozen or more non-medical missionaries who had taken a one week training course from Dr. Richard Buker in the early 1950's. They learned how to diagnose and treat leprosy. At that time people with leprosy were ostracized and rejected by their relatives. Missionaries giving physical care opened patients' hearts spiritually to hear the Gospel and many came to Christ. Mother and Dad were extremely busy with evangelism and village leprosy work. The medical practice at that time demanded that children be protected from contact with leprosy patients. So we kids had a choice of staying home alone all day or sitting in a hot car while our parents examined patients, gave out pills, trimmed elongated ear lobes and dressed ulcers. Neither choice was fun, but staying home was easier. However the long days without Mother and Dad were tiresome. I often made myself useful by baking for the family. Betty Crocker's cookbook became my companion as I filled the freezer with bread, rolls and Bonnie Butter Cakes.

Perhaps I inherited the intensity and drive for ministry from my parents' lifestyle. That and the normal stresses of adolescence contributed to poor health during my high school years. At one point I experienced strange and unexplained fainting spells. Dr. Ardel Vietti, the mission doctor in Vietnam, sent me to Saigon for tests. Then I was sent on to Bangkok for more tests. The doctors seemed to think I had a tendency towards epilepsy so

I was put on medication. Meanwhile I had missed six weeks of school. I hated taking the daily medicine; it seemed to be a reminder to me that I was sick. When my first bottle of pills was gone the nurse bought a refill of a local French brand. Within a couple of weeks I became so sleepy that one morning I couldn't wake up. The nurse rechecked my medicine and discovered this French brand was double the prescribed strength. Unintentionally I was being overdosed. This time when I used up the pills I didn't tell anyone. I simply quit—never to take them again.

My sophomore year of high school our family moved back to Korat a second time when Dad was elected the field chairman again. With the Vietnam War in progress the American military had stationed troops in Thailand. Korat was one of the big bases. The men assigned to the military field hospitals were bored with little to do since the war had not yet escalated, so they organized medical clinics to rural areas near the base. Three doctors and three translators would process 300 patients and call it a day's work. During summer and Christmas vacations from Dalat School Mother, Faith and I frequently assisted the American servicemen as the translators for the Thai villagers. I was pleased to have the opportunity to be involved in these medical safaris since it gave me a chance to experience medical work in anticipation of someday becoming a nurse. I also savored the military canned C rations; particularly the ham and lima beans were a treat. At Thanksgiving time we as a family were invited to three different US military camps and greatly enjoyed the American feasts!

May, 1962 was a tragic year in C&MA missionary history. We were on a family vacation at the beach in Thailand when word came of the abduction of C&MA missionaries Archie Mitchell, Dr. Ardel Vietti and Mennonite missionary Dan Gerber at the leprosarium in Banmethuot, Vietnam. Betty Mitchell with her children, Becky, Loretta and Glen had witnessed the Vietcong abductors taking their husband and father right before their eyes that night. Four year old Gerry in the crib in her bedroom was spared. No one knew what would happen to the captives or if there would be more kidnappings. Missionary colleagues all over Asia tensed up. Then they joined in prayer with supporters around the world imploring God for their release. The Mitchells had served as dorm parents at Dalat School and were well loved by all of us. As

21

MK's who naturally called them "Auntie" and "Uncle" it was as if our own father had been cruelly and suddenly snatched away. We cried and we prayed fervently. The new school year was due to open in only a couple of weeks.

Understandably, my parents did not want to send us children into a war zone when they themselves were in relatively safe conditions in Thailand. But this was to be my last year—the pinnacle of MK school life. All the Dalat kids looked forward to the senior privileges and the honors of finishing school. I, for one, certainly did not want to miss the climax! I begged my parents to allow me to return. With great reluctance they finally acquiesced.

My senior year at Dalat I was the school newspaper editor and kept busy with a variety of class activities. We ten seniors thought we were hot stuff! With a total of nine graduates from the previous years our class would more than double the Dalat alumni! [The year before in 1962 Jim Bollback and Nita Fowler had been the first graduates since 1953 when Thelmarie Roffe, Helen May Irwin and Urb Travis graduated.] We tried to mimic what American high schools did with special senior activities. We had class rings made and the local tailor made graduation caps and gowns.

However, the night before graduation, I was in a panic. Although I had chosen the title for my valedictorian speech a couple months before, I had not written even one word of the speech. It was 10 p.m., the time for mandatory lights out. I wanted to be alone—away from my three roommates. So I locked myself in the bathroom. I told God, "I just want to die! I can't face everyone tomorrow without a speech." My parents had driven three days from Thailand across Cambodia to Vietnam for the occasion. I was not thinking about committing suicide, I simply wanted to fall in a hole or disappear.

It was then that I realized I had been trying to live the Christian life in my own strength, and I could not do it. Right there alone in the bathroom I gave God full control of my life. Jesus was not only my Savior but now I was making Him Lord of my life as well. To my amazement I was able to write the speech in 30 minutes and then went to bed. I knew that it was not me—it was the Lord. At the graduation ceremony the next evening I knew

I was under God's control. I was totally calm and relaxed and gave the speech easily. It was the Lord who had taken control.

After graduation when our family drove back to Thailand Dad asked me to help in the mission office. He was the field chairman and his secretary had returned to America on a health leave, so my high school shorthand and typing courses were put to good use. Meanwhile I was awaiting word from the Los Angeles County General Hospital School of Nursing regarding my acceptance into the fall course. Finally I learned that my pre-entrance exams had not been received—evidently lost in the mail. The class was now full, and I would have to wait until next year for admission.

Without quite knowing why, I walked into Dad's office and said, "Well, Dad, I guess I'll be going to Simpson Bible College this fall." I knew nothing of their programs and had to write for a catalogue. At the same time New York headquarters wrote asking whether I would consider being a junior missionary for a year as my father's secretary. I really disliked secretarial work but I loved my Dad. I was in a quandary. What was God's will? Should I return to America not knowing whether or not I could get into college, or should I stay in Thailand another year as Dad's secretary?

I decided to return to America. Peace came to my heart immediately. I was reassured of His will from Proverbs 3:5-6: Trust in the LORD with all your heart and lean not on your own understanding; in all your ways acknowledge him, and he will make your paths straight. God had saved me spiritually and physically. He had called me to be a missionary. He had called me to be a nurse. I trusted Him for guidance, even though I didn't know whether or not I could get into college, I had peace about returning to my homeland without my parents. They would follow in a year when they completed their term of service.

4—Learning to Trust

"Ma'am this is a long distance phone call!" It was the School of Nursing at Los Angeles County General Hospital demanding an instant decision from me. My pre-entrance exams had finally arrived and they had a cancellation in the fall class that I could fill. Did I want to enroll for this year's class? I had just been accepted to Simpson Bible College in San Francisco and was planning to leave in two weeks. I was overwhelmed to have a choice between Bible college and nursing school. I realized God wanted me in Bible college first. I had lived a sheltered life as a missionary's kid. I needed to get reacquainted with my own American culture in a Christian atmosphere. "Thank you, but I'll wait until next year," I answered.

Now my problem was finances. According to the mission policy they would provide me an allowance for my first two years of college. But that $50 per month would not go very far. I had managed to save a total of $200 from all my birthday, Christmas and graduation gifts. Where would the rest of the $2,000 for one year at Simpson come from? I decided that if God was leading me to Bible school He would provide for my needs. And He did! The college gave me a 10% discount for being an MK. Then I did some baby-sitting. I also got a small scholarship from the Alliance Women in my church district. Then gifts, even from people I didn't know, started coming in and were credited to my account. By the time second semester came around the whole year was paid for, including an extra $50 a semester for pipe organ lessons! I found that God could be trusted for my financial needs.

Bible college living was not much of an adjustment for me since I had grown up in boarding school. My roommate was an MK who grew up in Western Australia where her parents ministered among aborigines. I was fascinated by her tales of kangaroos and throwing a boomerang. Another classmate was from Dalat, and we found that college was not much of a challenge academically, since we had been so well prepared by Dalat School. Although I dated occasionally in college as I had in high school I did not let my heart get interested in any fellow. I was determined to go to the mission field as a missionary nurse as soon as possible. No man was going to keep me from my goal. I knew that God had called me to be a missionary nurse—I would not be deterred.

After one year in Bible college I transferred down to Los Angeles for the three year nurses' program. Nursing school was a challenge academically and increased my personal confidence. Before I entered nursing I had asked the Lord, "Out of 450 student nurses, could I have at least one Christian friend?" He answered by giving me a whole organization—the Nurses' Christian Fellowship (NCF). Although some classmates took up smoking, loose living, marijuana and Ouija boards I found good friends and support in NCF. I learned to use Intervarsity's inductive Bible study method and went to NCF camps. I was thrilled to lead one of my classmates to Christ and witness to others.

I became a member of Hawthorne Alliance Church and taught a preschoolers' Sunday School class. One year for missionary convention we planned an international dinner. I volunteered to make Thai sticky rice with coconut custard. However I realized late in the week that I had never made coconut custard in my life, or even observed it being made. My parents were back in Thailand so I couldn't ask my mother for help. I had no recipe and could find no one with a regular custard recipe. Someone suggested eggs, milk and sugar, but in what proportions? I prayed for guidance and then mixed eggs, coconut milk and brown sugar together and set it in a pan of water in the oven. I had no idea what oven temperature or length of time was needed. When it was time for me to leave for church I found it was still soupy but I took it anyway. By the time I arrived at church it was "set" just right. I had not been a custard eater previously but when I tasted this, it was delicious! It was God's recipe. I discovered I could trust God for help in another area of my life--in the kitchen.

After completing my three year nursing course at the county hospital, I returned to San Francisco and Simpson to finish my degree. I agreed to be the college nurse to help pay my school expenses. On the weekends and during vacations I went on call with the Oakland Nurses Registry earning the handsome pay of $25 for an eight hour shift. As Bible college students we were required to participate in a Christian ministry in a church. So I taught a junior age Sunday School class at Tara Hills Alliance Church across the Oakland Bay. One Sunday night when I was

25

returning to the college alone, my tri-color Dodge sputtered to a stop on a deserted stretch of freeway. After desperately praying for God's help and multiple tries to restart the engine I decided I might need to walk down the highway in my high heeled shoes in the dark to find assistance. I hated the thought of leaving my new accordion in the car trunk. I tried one more time to start the engine and it was God's answer--the car took off without any problem. I was so elated that when I reached the toll booth to cross the Bay Bridge I breathlessly blurted out, "You'll never guess what happened! My car stopped for no reason and I prayed and God fixed it." The toll booth operator could only stare strangely at me. God proved to me that I could trust Him to be my mechanic as well.

My first year at Simpson in 1963 I had had a preliminary missionary candidate interview with Rev. W. W. Smalley of The Christian and Missionary Alliance Foreign Department. When I returned to Bible college in 1967 Rev. Robert Bartel was the Personnel Secretary in New York headquarters. He happened to be a shirt tail relative of mine (His father, Paul Bartel of China was Dad's first cousin). I met him for the first time when he came to Simpson for missionary candidate interviews. I told him I surely did not want any concessions made in any way on behalf of our blood relationship. For the theological aspect of the interview some Simpson professors were also present. A question was asked me relating to pre- and post-tribulation rapture of the Church. I looked at my teacher, Professor Len Wallmark, and said, "I don't know yet what I'm supposed to believe; we haven't come to that chapter yet." It brought a round of chuckles.

When I graduated from Simpson in 1968, The Christian and Missionary Alliance was ready to give me my final interview and assignment. But I realized that at 23 years of age I just didn't feel ready to go to the mission field. Having an "RN" after my name wasn't enough. I needed more experience. I was interested in midwifery and thought I would delay becoming a missionary by studying further. When I contacted the Frontier Graduate School of Midwifery in Kentucky, I was told there was a two year waiting list to get into the program. I did not want to wait that long but decided to go there and get some rural hospital experience. After training at what had been touted as the largest hospital in the

United States, I was now headed for a little 27 bed rural hospital tucked away in the hills of Kentucky.

Although I was accustomed to international travel, I was ill at ease traveling in my own country. Flying from Los Angeles to Louisville, Kentucky I discovered my connecting flight into Lexington had been canceled. However, the airline chartered a six seater plane to deliver us on schedule to our ticketed destination. It was an unexpected bonus from the Lord to fly so low over the beautiful horse farms with their white fences. In Lexington I went to the bus station where I struggled to understand the southern drawl spoken by the counter clerk. I spotted three other young ladies my age and discovered they were headed for the Frontier Nursing Service (FNS) in Hyden as well. Among the four of us we figured out where to get our Black Brothers bus which would connect us with a limousine in Manchester to take us to Hyden Hospital in the hills. In the final leg of the journey the limousine wound along the narrow road, barely missing dozens of coal trucks swerving down the highway. A blink and we would have passed Hyden town, it was so small. An FNS Jeep met us at the corner drugstore and took us up the hill to our living quarters.

Hyden Hospital was nestled in the lush Appalachian Mountains. The language sounded like old English to me. Four wheel drive Jeeps had just lately replaced horses for the nurses traveling up dry creek beds to visit their patients. Every nurse had to pass a harrowing driving test before the nursing service cleared us to drive. Being only 5 feet tall, I sat on an old telephone book to reach the pedals of the Jeep. My test was to drive up a creek bed until the boulders were too big to pass, and then back down! It was nerve wracking. But I passed. The local values ensured safety for us "outsider" nurses day or night. Our cottage had no lock on the door even if we had wanted to lock it.

In this mountain culture clan feuding was frequent. Often gunshot victims were brought to our emergency room. Our two doctors, both ladies, were capable of standing up to any drunk who threatened a nurse with a gun. Although the mountain people watched that first moon walk on TV in July, 1969 it was incomprehensible to many local people that it really had happened.

On the Sundays that I was off duty I helped teach adult Sunday School at Beefhide Gospel Mission in the small hamlet of

Essie. A delightful friendship developed with the Alliance workers and I learned much of the local culture through them. For Sunday dinner I could expect squirrel or possum with my potatoes and fried apples. It was a world of its own. I loved it.

Ordinarily at Hyden Hospital new nurses started work on the medical ward, but due to short staffing I was sent to work in the outpatient department and emergency room. This was ordained of God as it was the experience I needed. Within six weeks the supervisor approached me about being head nurse of the outpatient division because the head nurse was going to Africa as a missionary. I was overwhelmed and felt totally inadequate, but I reasoned that if I agreed to do as they requested it might increase my chances of entry into the midwifery training program. About a month after becoming head nurse, I was approached by the dean of the school of midwifery. "Joy," she began. "We've always had seven girls in the midwifery class but this November we want to start having eight. Would you like to be the eighth one?" God had answered my prayer. I could join that class after all. I was a month short of the required six months rural nursing experience and there was one small hitch. The midwifery program was followed by a three month internship but I was already scheduled to go to Toronto for the month of June for linguistic training. I would need to interrupt my internship and thus finish a month behind my class. This was permitted so I was "in." God had overruled the two-year-wait and arranged for me to cut in line.

The Kentucky mountains were in glorious autumn splendor when I flew out one weekend to meet the Foreign Missions Board for my final interview. New York State was just as gorgeous but arriving downtown at the bus station was frightening to me. Since it was Sunday night the hostess at Headquarters was in church and my phone calls were not heard until nearly 9 p.m. I stayed in the phone booth at the bus station pretending to talk on the phone as a ruse to keep strange men away. When I finally contacted the hostess she said, "Oh, just go out the door and down so many blocks...you are very near." Taking a deep breath, I stepped out of the phone booth with feigned confidence that I knew where I was going. An unsightly unshaven man stepped to the door insisting he was going to carry my suitcase. I reluctantly let go, reasoning that I could hit an assailant or run, more easily without the obstacle of my suitcase. I stuck close to the case and prayed hard until we reached 260 West 44th Street. Then I shoved a dollar bill at him and barged into the safety of the Headquarters. My hostess was waiting at the door. She apologized profusely for realizing too late that I was alone and it was night time. To me, the foreign field was safer than New York City!

At my interview the next day I found that all but one of the men had known me or my parents fairly well. Testing my determination to go to the field, the man who didn't know me asked, "Joy, what will you do if the board decides *not* to send you to the mission field?"

My unhesitating reply was, "I'll apply to the Overseas Missionary Fellowship board. I am just giving the C&MA first choice." We ended in laughter. Later I was asked if I would consider an appointment to Thailand as a nurse midwife in our leprosy work in Maranatha Clinic, Khonkaen. I was happy to accept! God had never specified a particular country to me—only that I was to be a missionary.

Back in Kentucky I began the midwifery course. For the first ten deliveries all eight students were required to observe the event. The babies seemed to have a propensity for night time appearances and we were called out at all hours. Sometimes it was more than once a night that we observed the miracle of birth. If I found the emergency room tough, this was even more stressful.

My classmates were mostly Lutheran nurses preparing to serve in Liberia and Nigeria. One nurse was a Baptist girl going to Pakistan and two other nurses were in their 50's, content to stay in America and practice midwifery. I was not accustomed to driving in the snow so in the winter I always made sure that my partner for home visits or home deliveries was a nurse who could drive on snow and ice. One of our more difficult routes was to the town of Thousand Sticks. In winter we nurses nicknamed it A Million Ruts, for obvious reasons.

At Christmas time I volunteered to take midwifery call since I could not go home for the holidays. I wished for a Christmas Day delivery only if it were necessary for such a mother to be in the hospital. Sure enough I was called. I put on red leotards under my green scrub dress to celebrate the season. (My British midwifery tutor later scolded me for looking so unprofes- sional!) Years later I reminisced to my sister's family. "Some where in Kentucky is a 20 year old man who was delivered by a midwife in red leotards and a green scrub gown. I don't even remember his name." Listening in, my four year old nephew piped up helpfully, "Oh, I know who, Auntie Joy, Colonel Sanders [of Kentucky Fried Chicken]!"

Opportunities came for me to visit a number of tourist spots in the state. I enjoyed an evening in an open amphitheater in Pineville watching the Book of Job dramatized. Another summer evening I was enthralled with The Stephen Foster Story, a musical drama playing near Louisville. And of course it was always fun to sit and chat with the local mountain people. Sarah Hall was a favorite with all the nurses. We were the best customers for her homemade corn shuck dolls, nativity figures as well as modern day characters. Then we all enjoyed the minor strains of music from hand crafted dulcimers. I stayed away, however, from the snake handlers in their churches. It was enough for me just to hear the nurses speak of the glazed eyes of the handlers. I had no desire to gawk at the demonic powers.

In June 1969 I flew to Canada to attend the month long Toronto Institute of Linguistics. It was a welcomed respite from the busy life in Kentucky. It also gave me an opportunity to renew acquaintance with faithful prayer warriors in the Avenue Road Alliance Church. The Hannahs were a group of women in this church who had prayed for a number of MK's, and I was one so blessed. The women were delighted that they could now pray for me as a new missionary. Some of them can testify to praying regularly for me for 50 years now. What a special blessing that has been.

In August that year I finished my midwifery internship in Appalachia. I returned to California to join my family who had just arrived for furlough from Thailand. I had only two weeks to prepare for leaving for my first term in Thailand. My parents were good experienced help in crating my bed, washing machine and filing cabinet and in packing the barrels with my belongings. The women of the Alliance churches had provided generously for the beginning of my missionary career. My outfit was a stark contrast to my parents' possessions right after World War II—one steamer trunk for our family of three.

My last Sunday in America was my commissioning in Hawthorne Alliance Church where I had my membership. Marthena Ransom, a retired C&MA missionary to India who was a member there was asked to give the charge to me. She revealed that when she retired she had asked the Lord for 12 young people from our church to be missionaries or full time workers. "And Joy is the first one," she said in praise to God.

Our newly installed pastor stood up and said, "I'm new here and don't know anyone yet. I wonder if there are other young people God has called to serve Him. Would you just stand up so I can see who you are." Exactly 11 more young people came to the altar. Marthena saw her 12 before her eyes and excitedly jotted our names down immediately. There was hardly a dry eye in the congregation as everyone marveled over God's working. Over the next years Marthena prayed faithfully for each of us. She challenged and reprimanded us as needed. She wrote to us on our birthdays and at Christmas. About ten years later it was noted that 11 of the 12 of us were serving the Lord overseas or at home. Marthena went to be with the Lord in February, 1988 after some two decades as a faithful prayer warrior. I felt the loss keenly, as though a piece of me were somehow missing.

The day after my commissioning I flew from Los Angeles to Hawaii for an overnight layover before continuing on to Hong Kong and finally, Bangkok. It was only a short three day trip compared to my parents' 32 day journey by ship 23 years earlier. My parents had learned to trust the Lord through hardships, limited income, sickness and uncertain situations. As a child I felt secure and loved. I never recalled feeling underprivileged. Living overseas was normal. My college years were just the beginning of learning to trust the Lord for my own needs. Whether for financial needs, friendships, education or safety I could trust Him. Yes, even for coconut custard or a stalled car—He was there.

5—A New Role

September, 1969. I was now a missionary, not just a missionary's kid. But I still only felt like "Joy" –nothing special or different. I was 24 and had been away from Asia only six years for my college education. The Thai culture, language, people and food were familiar to me. My adjustment however, was one of a role change. As MK's we all called missionary adults "Uncle" or "Auntie." Suddenly I was a colleague and wondered how I should address people. My question was answered immediately as a missionary gave me a big hug and said "Don't you dare call me 'Auntie.'" We were now coworkers.

Not so easy to decide was how the Thai Christians, particularly those who had known me as a child, should address me. It was the custom that missionary men and women were addressed using their last name. That would have brought confusion in referring to my mother as *Ma'am Boese* and me as *Ma'am Boese* also! I therefore suggested that I could go by my first name *Ma'am Joy*. In Bangkok this was becoming acceptable, particularly for single women.

Since I was the first MK to return to Thailand, no one had any idea how long language study might take me. Obviously the normal two years would not be necessary. I was able to speak Thai, but I couldn't read a word of it. The head teacher of the language school became my private tutor in the basics of reading until I could fit into an existing class. There are 44 consonants and 44 vowels in the Thai alphabet. The five tones were no problem for me to mimic as I had grown up with them. I was perplexed, however, on several occasions when a teacher corrected me on words I was sure I had pronounced accurately. Another teacher took me aside one day and said, "I'm from Khonkaen. That's the way you say it in the northeast. Here you have to learn Bangkok Thai." And then I understood. I had grown up speaking the northeastern dialect.

After ten months of study in Bangkok I was able to pass the final second year Thai language exams. This was followed by government exams for nursing and midwifery. Completing these

Maranatha Bible School was the only known leprosy Bible School in the world. The campus included teachers' homes, men's and women's dorms, dining hall, classrooms and chapel. In addition there was a rice mill, chicken coops, and hand crafts building. Although funds from the American Leprosy Mission subsidized the program the students were expected to work several hours a day to help pay their expenses. Their varying degrees of handicap or deformity determined their assignments. Missing fingers prevented some from doing the hand crafts. Some gathered coconuts from the trees lining the grassy driveway. Monkey-shaped money banks carved by the students from mature coconuts were a popular sale item. There was also intricate cross stitch and embroidery of Thai design on pillowcases and dresser scarves. Other students fed the chickens and collected the eggs for market. Leafy mango trees interspersed with straggly custard apple trees provided fruit, but the main crop was rice.

The resident farmer coordinated the annual cycle of plowing, sowing and harvesting. Although the 30 acres were timed to ripen consecutively, it sometimes happened that many fields were ready for harvest at once. A work day would then be declared and school closed. All the students and staff would head for the adjacent golden fields with crude iron sickles honed to a criminal sharpness. We missionaries too would join in. For us it was more of a diversion than labor.

We nurses would pull on long sleeved blouses and slacks or Thai wrap around skirts. We draped a multicolored all purpose cloth over our heads and necks to protect us from razor sharp rice blades. We would head for the fields and work from 6:00 to 7:00 o'clock and hurry home to shower and have breakfast. Slipping into white uniforms, we walked briskly down the dirt road to the clinic for the 8:00 o'clock devotional time. After clinic hours we could spend another short shift in the rice fields just before supper.

The students always loved to have us in the fields, even if we didn't lay the handfuls of cut grain just right, or cut the stalks too short or too long. "Watch your neck, ma'am," they warned me on more than one occasion as I awkwardly drew the sickle too near my head. I was five feet tall and the rice was unusually high that year. The rice heads swayed several inches above my blonde hair.

Each missionary household trained a village girl or woman to cook, bake bread, market and do house cleaning. House help was both a blessing and a bane; sometimes a trial but always a necessity. We depended on them in order to give our full time and energies to ministry. On the other hand, the helper's concept of cleanliness and consistency often contrasted with our own. For example, each evening the village buffalo lumbered down the dirt road dividing the Bible School campus from the mission homes. Clouds of fine brownish red dust would waft into our screened bedrooms and dining rooms. Each morning the helper was to sweep and dust the film of earth from the furniture and the floors. Missing the corners for a week or dusting around items most days was tolerated even though the helper knew better. But when the helper was inconsistent in following the bread recipe that was another matter! There was no bakery nearby or corner store in the village to buy bread, if there were a flop in the kitchen!

A second worker could be employed part-time to push the manual lawnmower and tend to the flowers and pineapple plants. One day we came home to find the yard helper relaxing in a wicker chair while watering the poinsettias. Why stand when you can sit? Because the helpers were totally unacquainted with electric machinery one of us nurses rose early to do the week's laundry using our wringer washer. We never let him touch the wringer as stories of other helpers' mishaps were recalled. There had not been just the broken zippers and the lost buttons but on occasion a whole arm getting drawn into the wringer! In spite of the local taboos that men generally don't touch women's clothing our male helper was willing to string our washing up on the clothesline.

Our clinic was always closed on Wednesdays since the government hospitals were open. (But we were open on Saturdays when the other institutions were closed.) Wednesday was thus our day off, unless we were on call. All our personal business in town had to be slotted into that day. However marketing was on Tuesdays except when it was a Buddhist holy day and no meat would be sold in the open air market.

On Monday night each household wrote a market list of items needed for the following week—beef for grinding into burgers, tomatoes and vegetables in season, fruit, flour and lard for baking, kerosene for fridge and stove, charcoal... and money enough for the purchases. We had a system—the four missionary homes (doctor, nurses, Bible school teachers) rotated the driving schedule.

So Tuesday morning at 5:30 sharp, the designated driver quietly unlocked their chained back door, gave a muffled greeting to the watch dog and tiptoed down the bare wooden stairs to drive the Land Rover or Isuzu truck. Then we slowly drove down the dirt road in the pre-dawn darkness to the village edge where the household cooks were waiting with their assortment of market baskets.

Half an hour later in town the cooks scattered among the fresh food stalls like ants gathering their morsels. Woe to any who overlooked an item on her list. It would be a week before she could get it. [Unexpected meal guests at Maranatha could cause a panic. Rice, fresh eggs and plucked chickens could be purchased from the Bible School. And some fruit and vegetables were available for sale in season from the school gardens.] The missionary driver had but one hour to run a list of errands compiled by all his colleagues. Yes, the photo shop near the market was open at 6:00 a.m. to pick up the reprints. Telegrams had to be sent at the side door of the post office. Always there was the stop at Central Bible School campus to pick up the week's mail and leave letters to be registered or an order for postage for next week. Sometimes there was a chance for a cup of coffee and to exchange news with a missionary at the campus. There were no water, gas or phone bills to pay because our only public utility was electricity. The vehicle might need fuel. The rule was never to come home with less than half a tank of gas.

Then it was pulling up to the market again before 7:00 a.m. and cramming the cooks and a virtual supermarket into the truck bed. A 30 minute dash down the highway, and the market was quite literally dispersed into the missionary homes at Maranatha. The driver had a quick shower, dressed and inhaled breakfast. Our typical market day breakfast was Chinese donuts dipped in sweetened condensed milk, and sticky rice topped with coconut custard. It was a rush to be at the clinic by 8:00 o'clock. Market driving was not one of my favorite jobs and I was always glad when my turn passed. I could sleep until 6:00 a.m. and have a proper quiet time with the Lord.

Changing from the role of MK to missionary there was one thing that continued. I had a bag of fears. When I was in language study in Bangkok our apartment seemed to be infested with cockroaches. A great big filthy creature would make an appearance in the living room and I would run from the room squealing uncontrollably. I knew it was silly but somehow it always got the better of me. My apartment mate was a new missionary from Pennsylvania. She would have to kill it. How ridiculous it was that I, the MK who had grown up with roaches, had to rely on her.

But that wasn't all. I had unreasonable fears of scorpions, snakes, and spiders. One day in conversation with Dr. Bare, our mission physician he mentioned how his wife had also had multiple fears when they first came to Thailand. He testified how God had delivered her. I thought to myself, *Good! God is the same today.* I prayed asking God to deliver me of these fears and named them to Him. Nothing happened. I decided, *Okay, this is my cross to bear on the mission field.* About a year later, quite out of the blue, God showed me the source of these fears.

One time when my sister Faith was an infant we were traveling on an overnight train. Several times she would awaken and whimper, and Mother would lift the netted baby basket to see what was wrong. No cause was apparent until she suddenly discovered a cockroach nibbling on Faith's delicate baby forehead. Ever after that I had a fear of roaches even though I had never been sampled by such creatures.

Then as a grade school student in Dalat, Vietnam, a large black hairy spider had perched over a bathtub in the girls' dorm. A helpful classmate had offered an encouraging bit of information. "It could be a black widow spider. If it bites you, you will die." It was likely a non-malicious species. But I carried a fear of spiders from that time on, terrorized by even threadlike daddy longlegs.

Then there was a missionary man who had the misfortune of sitting down on a scorpion that rested on a wooden toilet seat in a poorly lit bathroom. The result was a painful sting. Hearing that story I had glanced at every toilet seat for 15 or more years and fortunately was never similarly rewarded.

Being in a Buddhist country the Thai people generally scare snakes away rather than kill them. The belief in reincarnation dictates that any creature could be a deceased relative, depending on their karma and merits. For missionaries living in such a culture we simply could not always adhere to the policy of "let live." Deadly cobras were a regular menace to missionary children. I remember many occasions when Dad had to kill them in our yard. Other times when we drove the Jeep down red washboard roads at night the headlights would reveal a hooded cobra on the path.

In a flash I saw these roots of my fears. God then answered my prayer of one year before and delivered me from the fear of these creatures. I still did not like them but my irrational fear of them was gone. On night calls out to the clinic I had carried an oversized flashlight to watch the narrow path for snakes. If a blade of grass brushed against my foot, I'd jump six inches thinking that it was a snake. When God took the fear away I could walk confidently with a normal flashlight. In fact, I even came to enjoy an occasional meal of snake!

Dr. Bare had been a member of the Siam Society and probably knew more than anyone about the 200 kinds of snakes in Thailand. Only five of the species were said to be poisonous. He had also learned that python meat was a delicacy. When a villager came by with a dead python for sale the doctor eagerly purchased the prize and made a python lemon grass soup. He sent portions around for all of us to try. The snake meat tasted similar to chicken and pork, but the dozens of ribs alerted you that it was neither one.

Another reptilian favorite was lion snake toasted over a charcoal fire. In one village where we went to visit, the people gleefully prepared the doctor's favorite. When we sat around on the grass mat on the floor to eat our lunch we each had a stick of barbecued small frogs and pieces of lion snake. For me the snake and sticky rice, eaten with our fingers were delicious, but the frogs were another matter. I couldn't stomach those wee dead eyes staring vacantly at me. I whispered, "Dr. Bare, can you eat my frogs?" To my great relief, he unobtrusively took the frogs from my plate.

Our Maranatha Clinic existed not only to meet medical needs of leprosy people but also as a tool for evangelism. A crisis of health seemed to be God's means of penetrating traditionally calloused hearts in this country. A favorite event for all of us was a clinic trip about every other week, when half the staff would go to a village to visit a patient who had come to Christ. We all looked forward to our turn on the traveling team. Sometimes we held clinics for villagers. Other times it was more of a visit to the individual.

I recall one trip that took us, seemingly, to the end of the world. We usually bought rice and chicken to eat in a nearby town before reaching our destination or carried our lunch with us. Somehow this time we arrived at the patient's abode—a small shack in the middle of a rice field—without having stopped to buy anything. It was well past lunch time and we were quite hungry. No one expected the poverty stricken patient to feed us.

I discovered that all we had with us was a small basket of sticky rice and a little container of vegetable stir fry. I knew it was sufficient only for my missionary co-worker and me. What would the five Thai adults eat? God nudged me to bring it out anyway. I can't tell you how it happened. I only know that God multiplied the meager lunch somehow to fill the seven of us. We all ate until we were full and there was still some left over. I found God could be trusted to expand our food.

Then I recalled how many times as a teenager I'd seen God do the same thing. My parents had opened their home to American servicemen in Korat where Dad was field chairman in the early 1960's. Although our missionary budget was not adequate for hospitality on such a scale, God provided for the people He sent. The loaves of bread and meat and potatoes prepared to serve a dozen people filled five times that many hungry men. Again my childhood experiences had prepared me for the transition from MK to missionary.

6—Peas in the Fruit Salad

It was Christmas vacation and my two youngest sisters knew something that I didn't know. Dalat School, which had moved from Vietnam in 1965, was now in the Cameron Highlands of Malaysia. The school nurse was due for her year's furlough in mid 1971, and I was being considered by the school board as the one to replace her. It was strange that somehow everyone seemed to know about it except for me!

The visa situation in Thailand at that time was such that every ten or eleven weeks I would receive an urgent telegram from Bangkok saying "Your visa is expiring. You have 24 hours to leave the country to renew it." Planning my life around ten week segments became the norm, but it was still unsettling when the word came each time. Living in northeast Thailand I usually hopped on a train and went north to the nearest border to Laos. I would cross the river in a small passenger boat and within an hour or so have my passport stamped at the riverside immigration office in Laos. Then I walked through the next door, was stamped "out" of Laos, and re-boarded the boat. Within the hour I was having my passport stamped "enter" back into Thailand with a new visa granted for another ten or eleven weeks' stay. Thinking about a possible one year assignment to Malaysia sounded like a nice break from the visa hassle! The consensus of the missionary leadership was that I could be released from the Maranatha Clinic for the year. They would manage fine.

It was another role change—from being a former student to being a staff member. I was replacing my childhood boarding school nurse. Leprosy nursing and midwifery had become very familiar and comfortable during that year in Maranatha. Now I was headed for a change. Could I, the only nurse, manage the wide variety of medical needs of 100 students and staff? How would I relate to my former principal, Mr. Roseveare and the teachers? I found to my delight that almost immediately I felt at ease switching from the formal "Mr." and "Miss" to "Carl" and "Katie." I marveled that they accepted me as a full coworker when only eight years before I had been a student in the school.

That summer the school was moved from the crowded quarters of Eastern Hotel in the highlands, which had served as the Dalat School for nearly six years, to Penang Island. As I joined the staff we all of necessity became instant carpenters, painters and jacks-of-all-trades bent on transforming the holiday military housing of "Sandycroft" to dormitories and classrooms. We took down walls and nailed up other walls. The dance hall became the chapel. In spite of working feverishly, we still had to delay the opening of school by a few weeks.

Each of us on staff had specific responsibilities. Dorm mother, Bobbie Reed, had the unenviable task of retraining the Chinese cooks from British cuisine to American tastes. Their limited understanding of the English language was sometimes a source of frustration. One day the cook reported to Bobbie that the Jell-O for lunch would not gel in time. Bobbie said, "Well, in that case serve ice cream for dessert." At lunch we were surprised to have a scoop of chocolate ice cream on our lemon Jell-O.

That whole summer the staff ate in the school dining room to give the cooks a chance to practice their culinary skills. Bobbie kept emphasizing that when the school kids came everyone would eat at once—not one table at a time like the restaurant style they were accustomed to when Sandycroft was still an Australian military rest and recreation center. Their heads nodded in apparent understanding. But the first day of school was nearly a disaster. One hundred hungry kids poured into the dining room for breakfast. The kitchen crew's eyes grew as big as saucers. The mammoth pot of oatmeal on the stove had not even begun to boil yet! It was Kellogg's to the rescue—not just the first day but several days that first week. Of course the kids preferred Corn Flakes to oatmeal any day, but cold cereal was a luxury item, too expensive to be daily fare.

After school started I was in the kitchen one forenoon preparing a meal tray for a sick student. The fruit salad looked a bit peculiar to me. On closer examination I discovered green peas among the cut up pineapple and papaya chunks. Walking over to check the menu board I saw the problem—somehow the ingredients of fruit salad had been written too close to the vegetable for the meal. "Bobbie," I called on the intercom "there are green peas in the fruit salad for lunch!"

42

"Peas??" came her surprised reply. It was now only minutes before the students would descend on the lunch tables. The kids had complained enough times about other strange dishes they had been served. We could not handle another episode. Four of us staff members frantically swooped down on the serving bowls of fruit salad and salvaged the vegetable from the fruits. There was no time to explain our strange behavior to the cooks who hadn't a clue why the kids would want to eat their cool fruit salad and hot vegetables separately.

Traditionally Friday was "late night" at Dalat School and special activities were planned by the dorm staff. The very first Friday night at our new location on the island was planned to be a beach party for the older students and a picnic at the monkey park for the younger ones. Some of our dorm staff had not yet been able to get their Malaysian driver's license. Coming from Thailand where driving was also on the left side of the road, I had gotten an immediate reciprocal license. So it happened that the first week of school there were only two of us dorm staff available to drive the VW vans. We started transporting the younger children to the park at 4:00 o'clock. Then the older ones had to be taken to the beach. Navigating the winding two lane roads to the beach I wondered if the steering wheel might break loose. The husky senior high school boys jealously itched to take the wheel from their pint-sized nurse. By the time the other driver and I had transported all the kids to their respective sites it was getting dark and time to bring the younger ones home. After that it was time to pick up the older students. By 9 o'clock I had made nine trips, stopping only to refuel and nibbling on an apple for my supper. I didn't feel safe driving any more and could not make the last two trips needed. My male counterpart had had no less strain. Just then the school board meeting finished for the evening and two more dorm fathers were free to take over the chauffeuring. It was a Friday night I would long remember--five hours behind the wheel! The acquisition of a school bus was not to be realized for some time.

As school nurse it was my responsibility to locate the medical professionals we would need. The school personnel did not know anyone in Penang. Besides making the Adventist Hospital our medical authority, we required a dentist, orthodontist, and eye doctor. Who were the professionals who could take on a case load of 100 expatriate pediatric patients? One by one we began to find them. There was a backlog of dental needs. Some of the MK's came from countries where dental work was not available. When the school was in the highlands dental services were not readily accessible either. So the "need a dentist" list was an arm's length. Every Saturday morning I drove a van load of a dozen kids downtown to the dental office. I rarely had only one child for any appointment—it would be three to the eye doctor and two to the orthodontist. It seemed to be a continuous stream.

With the school now located on an island rather than a mountain we exchanged cool rain every afternoon for warm days and breathtaking sunsets over the ocean. Only a stone and concrete sea wall separated the children from the waves. Medically I was challenged. With the ocean side location came new injuries— jellyfish stings, sea snake bites and stingray wounds. However, ironically I never had to deal with a most common emergency, broken bones. Kids seemed to fall out of trees or break a leg on my day off or when I was off campus. One family of boys seemed to have a propensity for breaking a bone. Finally the doctor inquired if there were any more boys in that family. "Tie them down," he advised.

One item of grave concern to me was that in all the card-board boxes marked "clinic" I had not found the children's medical records. The nurse had packed them in the highlands months before and now I was the un-packer. I had searched everywhere. I wrote to the nurse on furlough and all she could remember was that they were in a cardboard box. I was beginning to believe that the carton had been lost in the move. I was afraid to give even an aspirin to a child as I had no record of allergies or medical history. Then one day when I had a little free time I quite unexpectedly chanced upon them. I was unpacking the last boxes of clinic equipment and came to one marked "pots and pans for give away." There in the bottom were the important records I needed! How thankful I was to find them!

A first grade boy contracted measles about the first week of school. I had no clinic room in which to isolate him, so confined him to his mosquito net-draped bed and then cautioned his three roommates to only enter their room to sleep at night. But coming home from the dentist trip that Saturday I found a welcome surprise. The staff had emptied two storage rooms beside the clinic to make isolation rooms for sick students. The rooms had literally been crammed to the ceiling with spare foam rubber mattresses. What did they do with them? Each kid got a second mattress on his or her bed.

Then there was the eighth grade boy from Indonesia who gave me a note from his mother when he came for the new term. "Tim was exposed to mumps here. He's never had them so watch for symptoms." Sure enough, two weeks later he had mumps. In spite of the isolation room, we had mumps and more mumps passing from one student to another. When November came the student body began praying earnestly that God would stop the mumps epidemic. The kids knew that when school ended in early December, any child with mumps would be delayed from flying home for vacation. God answered their prayer and Thanksgiving Day saw the last case of mumps recovering.

Dengue fever was another illness I had to contend with. It was contracted through mosquito bites. The tropical warmth and daily afternoon thunder showers seemed to breed an extra supply of mosquitoes on campus. I was kept very busy fixing and delivering meal trays to all the dorms as there were too many sick students to stay in the clinic rooms. Then over Christmas vacation a polio epidemic hit the island. I telegraphed each mission field sending students to make sure the children were immunized before returning to school.

At the end of the school year I realized God had kept me healthy all year in spite of all the sickness among the students and staff. In a prayer letter, I praised the Lord for His health. But about a week later I came down with a cold! I was disgusted about it as there was no reason for it. It was a communion Sunday and the thought came to me that I could ask the Lord for healing. So as I took the communion cup I prayed, "Lord, could you please heal this cold?" I felt my sinuses drain. And on the second sip of grape juice I was healed. My two younger sisters, Carol and Melody were still in boarding school at the time and sitting beside me in church. Excitedly I whispered to the one next to me, "Carol, the Lord just healed me of a cold!"

A month later I was fighting a sinus headache. Again it was a communion Sunday. I recalled my healing from the cold the month before and prayed, "Lord, I trust You to heal this headache." But nothing happened. I thought to myself, *Never mind, God doesn't always heal immediately.* I went to a church elder in the afternoon and asked him to pray but that didn't bring relief either. By evening I was so miserable I had to go to bed. As I lay there on my bed I said, "Lord, I don't understand. I asked You to heal me but nothing has happened." Then it occurred to me that if I really believed He would heal I should thank Him in faith. I began to thank Him, and within a half hour I was well. *Whew!* I thought, *I should have thanked Him earlier.*

But the next morning I awakened with another sinus headache. God had given me the faith to believe Him for an acute problem of yesterday, but this was chronic. I realized I had just a little faith and I needed more. That day in my personal devotional time I came to the story of the man whose son had an evil spirit. Jesus told him to believe. The man answered, "I do believe; help me overcome my unbelief!" (Mark 9:24). I identified with that. "Yes, Lord, that part in which I don't believe—please help me."

The following day I read of the woman who had a bleeding for 12 years. God gave me the faith. I literally stretched out my hand to touch the hem of His garment. "Yes, Lord, I do believe." And I was healed. After years of sinus headaches God had brought relief. Healing was a natural expectation to me since I was a child. I could remember many times my parents praying for one of us kids. God's healing touch repeatedly proved His Word: "Ask and it will be given to you" (Matthew 7:7).

One school vacation there was a mix-up of the train reservations for the 30 students returning from Malaysia to Thailand. We were unable to get sleeping berths together for all of them in one train car. The group was to be spread out among five carriages for the 26 hour trip. Although two staff members were assigned to chaperone the kids home, at the last minute one was unable to get a visa. So I was left as the lone escort for the group. I wondered how I was going to keep track of so many kids scattered about for so many hours. So I began making assignments.

The senior girls drew first class sleeping compartments. I strictly ordered them that no one was allowed in the door of their room after bedtime. The older boys were assigned to sit up in the coach seats in the first and second class cars. The rest of the junior and senior high girls were assigned second class bunks with heavy pull back drapes.

Early in the evening I overheard two train stewards discussing their night time activities. They were unaware that I understood their language since this was an international train. So before bedtime I called the girls in second class bunks together and gave strict instructions. "If anyone tries to climb in your bunk tonight you yell and scream and I'll...." I didn't know what, but I would do something!

About 11:00 o'clock I was just dropping off to sleep when my worst fears were realized. Two girls were yelling, "Get out! Get out!" I jumped up to find my own sister and her friend sitting on a lower bunk terrified. They had opened their shuttered window to enjoy the stars just as the train had arrived at a station. A steward saw the open window and was trying to close it from the outside to protect them from rocks which might come in at night as the train wound up the mountain side. I finally got everyone calmed down.

In the day time I had another safety concern. The conductor complained to me that the boys were jumping off the train and in danger of being killed or left behind. I was puzzled by this report and went to investigate what was happening. The train was climbing at a considerable incline as we negotiated the mountain pass. With nothing more exciting to do to fill the long hours, some of the boys were jumping down the unlocked stairwells, picking up some small stones beside the tracks and hopping back on the train. Then they competed to see who could hit the most electric poles. When I pointed out that if they should get left behind I might never know until we reached Bangkok, they realized the seriousness of their pastime. They were excited to be reunited with their parents for Christmas and did not want to hazard a delay.

Approaching our destination in Thailand I foresaw another problem. I had 30 kids and literally 100 pieces of counted luggage to disembark at a five minute train stop in Bangkok. *How could we do it, being so scattered about the train?* I wondered. Then I formed a plan. I got the kids up at 6:00 o'clock and we began moving all the luggage to the second class bunks. All the students were given assignments. When the train stopped four older boys stood two to a window and tossed suitcases out to four boys who jumped out on the platform to receive them. The rest of the kids were lined up to march off both ends of the carriage with all hand luggage in tow. I stood in the middle to direct operations. I gave strict instructions, "No one is to hug their parents until all bags and people are off the train." It worked. The train station personnel didn't know what hit them. In five minutes—whoosh! 30 kids and 100 bags had descended on them. Vacation had now begun.

The staff of the Dalat School had made it through that hectic summer move of 1971 by learning to praise the Lord. As a group we had worked through Merlin Carothers' book *Prison to Praise*. And our busy pace never slackened through the school year.

It was early March, 1972 when Teo van der Weele a Dutch C&MA missionary to Thailand came to the school to speak for the spiritual emphasis week. Teo and his wife Wil were my good friends and I was delighted to see them. Teo was chatting with a number of us staff members and informally sharing about the gifts of the Holy Spirit. He could see that we were all overloaded and struggling to meet the demands of giving good physical, spiritual and emotional care to the missionaries' children. We had a crucial role in keeping both parents and children happy so that parents could fulfill their ministries.

"You need to ask the Lord for power tools," Teo said. "You don't have time for hours and hours of counseling the kids. Ask the Lord for a gift of knowledge to know what the problem is. Ask for a gift of wisdom on how to help." It made sense to me. *He's right,* I thought.

Teo then stated that his personal life was continuously re-charged by praying in tongues. As he shared I said, "You make me want to speak in tongues, Teo."

"Good," he said in his characteristic Dutch accent.

The spiritual emphasis meetings were challenging and thought provoking. But personally I felt like I was under a black cloud. I assumed I had grieved the Lord in some way and asked Him what it was. But nothing came to mind. I looked up scripture passages listing various sins but again nothing was revealed. Then I asked Teo and Wil to pray with me, thinking God might reveal it to them. Again it yielded nothing.

Then Teo asked, "Joy, did you ask the Lord for tongues?"

"Yes," I replied.

"Did you get it?"

"No." I didn't know what was supposed to happen.

"Well," he said, "I'll pray in tongues for you and then you pray out whatever sounds are in your heart." As he began to pray in flowing words I was fascinated. I had never heard anyone speak in tongues before.

"Teo, is that Hebrew?" I asked when he stopped.

"I don't know. You pray now." he instructed. Without stopping to question or reason it out, I began praying the sounds in my heart. Then I stopped. I didn't understand it.

It must be nothing, I thought. Immediately the interpretation flowed from Teo's lips—praise and worship to God. Instinctively, I knew deep in my spirit it was what I'd prayed in tongues. There welled up deep within me a fresh spring of spiritual water— bubbling and bubbling. In a word of prophetic affirmation Teo added, "My daughter knows my voice." The whole episode had taken place in just 15 minutes in my apartment.

It was now 3:30 p.m. and time for me to take two students to the doctor for ingrown toenail surgery. On the outside I looked the same. But in my heart there was a new line of communication. I felt like I was jabbering with a long lost friend catching up on years of time. I was unperturbed that the doctor's appointments meant a late supper for me. Everything seemed to have come into a deeper dimension. By bedtime I was saying, "Lord, could You please turn it off so I can sleep?" I concluded that the dark cloud of the previous days was evidently just a ploy of the enemy who had recognized my spiritual thirst and tried to thwart me.

In hindsight I realized I had had these sounds in my heart for many years. At times they bordered on deep groanings. After all, I had asked to be filled with the Spirit at an altar as an eighth grader, but no one had given me any further teaching. I knew Pentecostals spoke in tongues, but otherwise I was totally ignorant on the subject. I was neither for nor against speaking in tongues and had not even heard of the term "charismatic."

God used Teo to minister His blessing to many students and staff during that week. He reported that one MK from Vietnam had prayed in perfect Thai—a flowery language she had never learned. He laughed saying, "I didn't need any gift of interpretation for that. I just translated."

It seemed that I had known God the Father and his Son, Jesus all my life. But of the Holy Spirit I was quite ignorant. Suddenly I couldn't read enough about Him. That year I managed to read 40 books on the Holy Spirit. I began to realize it was a hot topic, even controversial for some Christians. I had fallen into it almost by accident, because I had no theological hang ups. It was a pivotal event which enriched and affected the rest of my life.

In Asian culture it is logical and not unusual to ask a person of means if you need or want a gift of some kind. Family members who earn a paycheck can expect to be approached for a handout. As a child of the God Who had gifts I needed, I too felt no compunction in asking my Father for the power tools I needed for ministry. I had asked for tongues for my personal edification. I also asked for knowledge, wisdom and faith. In the months that followed God proved his Word "Ask and it will be given to you" (Matthew 7:7).

As I was praying for the junior and senior high school students one morning in my devotions I was amazed to find very specific needs come to mind for each individual. I wrote them down, wondering if it was my imagination. But in the weeks and months that followed these items were confirmed one by one. The knowledge I received was obviously from a divine source. As students came to me for counsel I became aware that the answers I was giving were not my own but God's wisdom. It was as if God wanted me to personally experience His divine gifts to assure me they were still for use today.

It was after eight o'clock one night when I happened to pass by a second graders' dorm room and thought I heard someone crying. Opening the door I found a child sitting up in bed with a comb tangled in her blonde hair. I was puzzled why she was even awake an hour after being put to bed. "I wanted to look pretty for my queen," she whimpered. I ended up having to trim away some hair to get the comb free. Yes, Her Majesty Queen Elizabeth II was expected to tour Penang Island the next day. Everyone was excited and hoping to see her. Earlier in the day some other grade school children had informed me, "You are supposed to brush your teeth if you are Canadian in case the queen smiles at you."

The next day anticipation ran high as the Dalat School students and staff dressed up in their best clothes and lined both sides of the highway outside the school gate. The oldest Canadian student was given the honor of presenting an orchid bouquet to the queen should the royal motorcade be persuaded to stop. The Queen and Duke of Edinburgh *did* stop—perhaps out of curiosity regarding all these western children. But the excitement soon died down and even dissolved into disappointment. Several grade school kids said they only saw a pretty lady in a car—there was no elegant queen wearing a crown on her head! In my journal I wrote, "March 8, 1972 11:40 a.m. Queen Elizabeth II stopped at Dalat School. Jesus Christ, King of Kings, already visited each individual who desired an audience with him!!"

Besides my nursing responsibilities I had bedtime detail for girls grades three and four. Realizing that the MK's know most Bible stories by heart, I chose Brother Andrew's book, *God's Smuggler*. I improvised a paraphrase on the spot as I "read" it at their level. At one point they learned that tulip bulbs were eaten in Holland when the potatoes were in short supply. The little Dutch MK commented, "At least they didn't become extinct." (We didn't know if she meant bulbs or people!) Another of the eight girls marveled at the miracle of passing through [literal] iron curtains to distribute Bibles as well!

Listening to the prayers of the grade schoolers brought to mind how much missionary vocabulary they pick up. There was the fourth grade girl who prayed, "And Lord, please don't let me die until I finish my work. You know I haven't even started it yet." God must have chuckled knowing that He would lead her back to the mission field as an adult some twenty years down the road! These childish comments lightened many a day for me in my harried schedule.

A weighty decision was hanging over me. More dorm staff were needed at Dalat for the next school year. I had been asked if I would stay on the staff for a second year and be dorm mother to grade school girls. I had anticipated only a one year parenthesis from being nurse midwife at Maranatha Clinic in Thailand. I prayed for a couple of months asking for God's guidance. There seemed to me to be three or four signs pointing to my continuation on staff. Finally one day I sat on my bed and I petitioned, "God, what shall I do, stay in Dalat or return to Thailand?"

"Dalat," came the immediate clear word in my heart. Suddenly I was laughing at myself. I'd been asking God for an answer like a small child tugging on her mother's apron, "Mommy, Mommy, Mommy," but never stopping long enough to listen to His answer. When I stopped to listen, He spoke.

For my second year on staff I became dorm mother to eight first grade girls. I also shared responsibility with Charlie and E.G. Long for 30 high school girls. This new role brought out my mothering instincts. I especially loved the bedtime prayers and expressions of childish faith. My only regret was that *I* was the beneficiary of their verbal gems while their own parents far away had to sacrifice that joy. As much as possible I tried to relate such precious and hilarious moments in notes to their parents. After these two years on staff in the Dalat School I felt as though I had done my share of child rearing for a lifetime!

Since my nursing school days in Los Angeles I had been involved with Nurses Christian Fellowship (NCF) in each country where I lived. I attended Malaysian NCF camps and knew a number of the Malaysian, Chinese and Indian nurses. One morning during my personal devotions the Lord impressed on my heart that I was going to speak at the next nurses' retreat. It was so clear that I knew, whether or not the committee invited me, I would have to go prepared to speak. I thought maybe at the last minute a speaker would break a leg or whatever and I'd be asked to speak in that person's place.

With this clear knowledge I wrote MNCF saying I wanted to attend the retreat this year but I needed to know the dates so I could request my semester's five day break for that time. A reply came back with an added comment, "Next week the committee is meeting to decide on the speakers and program. Please pray for God's guidance." I chuckled to myself.

I was not surprised to get a letter soon afterwards asking if I would be one of two speakers. But the topic I was assigned *did* surprise me. I was to spend two one hour sessions on "The Holy Spirit and the Nurse." It was a delightful challenge. My written response confirmed what God had told me before they asked. Furthermore I'd read 40 books over the past year and would love to share the blessing I'd received. I was keenly aware of the Lord's anointing on His assignment at that nurses' conference.

After the school year was over I attended another conference in Malaysia. The housing was a bit crowded and so thirty of us ladies were lined up on cots dormitory style in one room. There were no screens on the windows and no nets over the beds. And there was only *one* ceiling fan in the whole room. My bed was not even *near* it! From past experiences, I knew I was going to be a prime attraction for hungry mosquitoes. The inevitable happened. That night as I tossed on the cot and swatted buzzing mosquitoes, a thought came to me. *Lord, You created these mosquitoes. Could You please keep them away from me so I can sleep?* I asked. He did so and I slept.

The next morning, however, the other ladies complained bitterly of how they were chewed up by the flying bombers. *They can pray for their own mosquitoes!* I thought smugly. But God reprimanded me. *He* had given me the faith to ask Him so *I* needed to pray for them. On retiring that night I asked my Heavenly Father to protect my roommates from the mosquitoes as well.

The next morning I hesitantly asked the lady in the next cot, "How did you sleep last night?"

"Fine."

"No mosquitoes?"

"No mosquitoes." God had answered.

At the end of the conference week I went to pack my bag. As I gathered my clothes from the open dress rack at one end of the room swarms of mosquitoes flew up in my face. *Aha,* I thought. *That's where the Lord banished them to!*

Just moments later an Indian girl came in and sat on a bed beside me. "This is a strange city," she commented. "There are no mosquitoes." I looked at her and then related how God had taken control of them.

Returning to Thailand some weeks later I related my mosquito story to a missionary colleague. A couple of nights later we were both seated at the back of a meeting room where her husband was preaching. The mosquitoes were having a great feast at our expense. We swatted and scratched and slapped mechanically.

Then she leaned over and whispered to me, "Joy, you ought to pray for these mosquitoes!" Suddenly I felt my faith was on the line. But then I thought—*She's right. We can't concentrate on the message.*

"Father, would You please take these mosquitoes away?" I silently prayed. Presently, I realized the mosquitoes were gone. I happened to look behind me. There on the wall were tens of mosquitoes perched quietly. I nudged my missionary colleague, "Look," I said.

"Did you pray for those mosquitoes?" she asked excitedly.

"You asked me to," I replied. Yes, I could trust God to provide for my creature comforts. After all He created the mosquitoes.

Although I was due to go on my one year furlough I wrote a request to the mission asking to extend my term on the field for another five months. Having been in Malaysia for the last two years where I did not use the Thai language it seemed advisable to refresh my verbal skills back at Maranatha Clinic in Thailand. A second reason for my request was that it would enable me to overlap my time in America with my parents' furlough for six months rather than miss them altogether.

Back in Maranatha in Khonkaen, Thailand the routine of clinic patients was in full swing. It was a surgery day so I was examining outpatients and weeding out the simple cases to lighten the doctor's load. By noon time the surgery case was still not finished so I began to scrub in to relieve the surgery assistant for lunch. Suddenly I was overcome with strange abdominal pains. The intensity increased to the point that I could hardly stand up and a fellow missionary had to walk me down the short dirt lane to my home. Soon I was writhing in waves of sheer agony. At the same time my colleague and I were praying for my relief. In a flash I sensed that a spiritual dimension was somehow involved and urged, "Rebuke the devil!" My colleague did so in the name of Jesus and instantly the abdominal storm ceased. I felt drained and perplexed by the whole ordeal. We realized there was a spiritual battle raging. We pled the blood of Jesus over the surgery at the clinic where we heard the patient was unexplainably going into shock. A fairly simple surgery had stretched to several hours beyond what was expected.

"Joy, what happened today to give the devil a chance?" questioned my colleague as we sat together in my home. I didn't have a clue. Then we recalled that there had been a peculiar woman patient that morning. She was large boned and husky voiced and we later realized that "she" was in fact a man. I remembered examining "her" eyelids for signs of anemia and experiencing a strange, almost imperceptible shiver of fear go through me. Later our Thai receptionist told us this transvestite had been a powerful spirit doctor from her former village. Ten years before, previous to becoming a Christian, our employee had been under his demonic powers. The Thai explained that this spirit seemed to reproduce "junior" spirits that would attach themselves to others. When this patient had appeared at the registration window she had recognized him and asked if he remembered her. He didn't. It was a confirmation to her that the Spirit of Jesus within her now had no connection whatsoever with the former powers that had controlled her as a non-Christian.

With this knowledge things now began to make sense to us. The previous evening the missionary nurse on call had been summoned over to the clinic to arrange sleeping accommodations for this "woman" and other patients in the outpatient rooms. She'd come home and said to us, her house mates, "You guys, I don't know what's wrong. I feel strange. I can't explain it." We had simply prayed a cleansing and protection over her by the blood of Christ and went to bed unaware of the cause of the problem.

"Please," we entreated our Thai staff, "let us know when you are aware of patients with demonic powers. We foreigners are so ignorant of these things. What is commonplace to you is unknown to us."

In the missionaries' prayer meeting the next evening I testified to the Lord's deliverance from this demonic attack. I admitted I didn't know where that fear came from. Then I requested my fellow workers to lay hands on me in prayer and ask God to deliver me from all fears. They did so.

The following week I was to teach a Thai women's group. Ordinarily getting up to speak before a public audience would ensure I would have a batch of butterflies hatching in my stomach. As a teenager I had become physically ill and sometimes unable to meet my obligations when I had to speak publicly. But this time I was baffled and thrilled to find that I was not the least bit nervous in teaching the women. Then it dawned on me. As my coworkers had prayed for me God had delivered me from the fear of public speaking! How timely it was when I was facing my first furlough with its dozens of speaking engagements on missionary tour!

Finishing my first term as a missionary, I had two concerns on my mind as my plane touched down in Los Angeles three days before Christmas in 1973. I wanted to attend the Urbana Student Missionary Convention in Illinois the next week, and I had no warm clothes! I had had my sister mail me a winter coat from Minnesota. She chose a striking velvety purple one—not wanting me to look like a dowdy missionary! But I wondered how I would manage to shop for other warm clothes in California during the peak of holiday madness.

God prepared the perfect solution. A deaconess from my home church said, "Joy, aren't you headed for Urbana in a couple days? Would you like to borrow some warm clothes for your furlough year?" It was just an ideal arrangement. She had three daughters about my size and I was soon outfitted with snow boots, sweaters and hat. The items would be returned at year's end since I'd have no use for them in Thailand's humid tropical heat.

My second concern was transportation to Illinois. I found that God had reserved the last seat for me on the bus Intervarsity had chartered from Los Angeles. When I had left for the mission field four and a half years before I had been asked, "How does it feel to be a missionary?" I didn't feel anything and I still didn't. I was just me. I was not a spiritual giant as the missionary predecessors I idolized. But as I boarded the bus for the three day trip with 49 college students I questioned *their* view of me. I wondered whether I was still on their wave length. But I didn't have long to wonder. Somewhere in Arizona or New Mexico as we rolled along the highway the bus microphone was handed to me to share God's blessings on the mission field. I felt totally at ease.

Within minutes of our bus arriving on the university campus in Illinois I bumped into my missionary colleague. It was God's timing as I recalled spending three days searching for my sister when I attended Urbana '67. This time there were twice as many people registered—some 14,300. As missionaries we were there to interact with the students. We were picking our way through a throng of youth when I heard someone say, "The Christian and Missionary Alliance." I turned immediately to see two youngish unfamiliar faces. I knew you had to know someone in the C&MA to even say the word. "Where are you from?" I began.

"Canadian Bible College," he answered.

"Oh good. What is your major?" I continued. The lady beside him quickly answered,

"He's the president."

"Oh, nice to meet you—and this is your wife?" She wasn't. It was Dr. David Rambo and another college representative. I chuckled but felt as though I had opened my mouth and inserted both feet!

Preparing for my first missionary speaking tour in February, 1974 I laboriously made a cassette tape of the script for my slide presentation. A seasoned missionary had recommended I do so in case I lost my voice in a conference and couldn't speak. At least a church could have something as a stand-in, she had suggested.

My first missionary conference was in Washington state. As I nervously walked in the church door prepared to speak for the church worship service, I was accosted by the Sunday School superintendent. "Miss Boese, we'd like to have you speak to our Sunday School as well." I was momentarily unnerved. They hadn't told me this beforehand. Within minutes I was introduced as a gift of the Spirit—"Joy" and God proceeded to fill my mouth.

Slides were scheduled for that first evening service. Being a novice and unsure of myself I decided to use the taped script rather than live monologue. It went so well I never did do it live in spite of the periodic background hum of the heater clicking on in the bedroom where I had done the recording!

The churches of the Pacific Northwest District were sometimes hard pressed that year to transport the missionaries crisscrossing Washington, Oregon and Idaho. It was the winter of the gas shortage. Cars with even numbered license plates were allowed to buy gas on alternate days from those odd numbered plates. There were long lines of cars at the gas pumps. One memorable event for me occurred in Redmond, Washington when my hostess, Bobbie Reed, was to drive me north to Burlington. We awakened on Sunday morning to an unexpected blanket of one and a half inches of snow on the ground. As we left her home we prayed for a gas station to be open on our route as her fuel was running low. We made a wrong exit from the highway but at the bottom of the ramp was a gas station! And it was open! We praised the Lord that it was the right exit by God's plan, and thankfully filled the tank. Later that afternoon we happened to pass the same station and doubly thanked God for His timing. The gas was now gone, the station was closed!

As a woman I always felt an extra pressure when I spoke for a Sunday morning worship service. Our instructions from the mission headquarters were that we should report on the foreign field—we were not to preach. That was the pastor's job. I wholeheartedly agreed. I was a nurse and only had two years of Bible college. I was not trained to preach. And yet I knew that for many churchgoers their only spiritual feeding for the week was what they heard in the pastor's sermon on Sunday morning. So I always made sure there was a scriptural setting and application to my messages.

I also had a personal prejudice against women preachers. I knew God used them but I personally preferred to listen to a man in the pulpit on Sunday morning. I also knew that pastors were at the mercy of the district tour schedule. If the lady missionary were assigned to their church for Sunday morning they'd have to do something with her. Secondly, God calls all kinds of people to be missionaries to serve Him. Some are especially gifted in literacy work or personal one-on-one ministries. Public speaking can be a nightmare to some men as well as many women missionaries. So it is usually a step of faith for the pastor to schedule the missionary speaker he doesn't know. He just trusts that the missionary man or woman will communicate well to his congregation.

Sitting on the platform moments before I was to speak one Sunday morning in Oregon, the pastor leaned over to me. "You are the first woman in this pulpit for some years. The last lady missionary broke down and cried in the pulpit so an elder has refused to allow women speakers on Sunday morning since. But he is out of town today." I really didn't need to hear that! The added pressure of breaking a mindset made me thrust myself upon the Lord's help more than ever. I was weak but He was strong.

That first speaking tour ended in Bly, Oregon and I flew out of Klamath Falls in an April snow storm! Arriving in San Francisco I was to see my brother, Tim at Simpson College. When I got to the doorstep of his apartment I was greeted by one of his three house mates. He looked me up and down and then blurted out, "But you don't *look* like a missionary! I thought missionaries were old ladies with hairy legs who didn't wear nylons." At 29 years of age in a pant suit I didn't fit the description.

In May that year I was going to attend annual council in Georgia. En route from California I stopped in Lexington, Kentucky. Somehow the Greyhound bus had sent my suitcase to Lexington, *North Carolina*. My missionary slides, black notebook of messages and everything I needed was in that suitcase. I was told it would be at least a day before the suitcase could possibly catch up to me at the next stop. So I had no option but to commit the problem to the Lord. God had a hidden blessing in this small trial. The next day I had an hour's wait in a small Appalachian town before my hostess could retrieve me from the bus station. With no bag and nothing to do I decided to walk around. Beside the bus station was a little dress shop. To my utter delight there was a darling white summer suit just my size on sale for half price—only $14.00. God knew my personal dislike for shopping and had to take away my suitcase so I'd buy a suit! An hour later my bag caught up with me. His timing and ways are perfect. He does have a sense of humor!

Mid August saw me in St. Paul, Minnesota for the very first seminar to be held for missionaries going on speaking tour. We were briefed on how to conduct ourselves as representatives of the C&MA. Our job was to challenge the constituency to "pray, give, and go." Missionary conference was the C&MA church's heart and the highlight of the year. We needed to hone our presentation skills for maximum performance. A new technique was taught—making cassette tape scripts to go with our slide presentations. Interestingly enough God had already led me to do that very thing.

Part of this workshop was critiquing each other's slides. A colleague from Irian Jaya was taking her turn. One of her slides was a washed out pale green picture with a tiny yellow spot in one corner. "This is a bird that appeared one day last year on our island. We've never seen it before and we don't know what it is. Next picture." A roar of laughter erupted from the missionary audience. She had just broken every rule of good slides and commentary. Dr. L.L. King our Foreign Missions Secretary later admitted he was laughing so hard he nearly fell out of the college's balcony.

My first furlough ended after a nine week fall tour in my own district of southern California. God had led me through many lessons of learning to lean hard on Him and trust Him in every circumstance.

9—Tornado

I returned to Thailand for my second term by way of Europe. I was among 250 passengers squashed into the plane from Switzerland. An Austrian lady sitting beside me coughed her bronchitis germs around quite generously the whole trip. We had an hour and a half stop in Tehran, Iran. A heavy snowstorm there had caused the airport terminal's roof to cave in. As a result melting snow dripped everywhere in the building. As passengers we walked around uneasily looking at the unsmiling guards who were armed with rifles. Arriving in Bangkok many hours later was a shock to my body. Europe's snowy sub-zero temperatures were replaced by Asia's sweltering 90's even in December. It was no wonder that I spiked a fever within a couple of days.

Illness for a single girl can be frightening. I found myself unexplainably on the bedroom floor twice before breakfast. Then it dawned on me that I must have fainted. Taking my temperature I found it was 104 degrees. I was thankful to still be at the Alliance Guest Home in Bangkok rather than alone out in a province.

Back in the groove of nursing at Maranatha Clinic once again I sensed a growing dissatisfaction in my heart. I had a strong desire to evangelize and witness verbally. Although we capitalized on every opportunity to share the Gospel in our medical ministry, it wasn't enough. My spirit longed for more.

In the coming year I knew our mission staff was changing shifts. The doctor was due to go on a one year furlough again and no one knew who would be his replacement. Our Canadian head nurse was also leaving for furlough and anticipated an extended home leave to care for her elderly mother. The nurse was a super capable woman with many years of experience running a one person clinic. She seemingly worked circles around the rest of us. The Dutch physiotherapist had trained a national to do the rudimentary skills of her trade before leaving for Holland on her furlough. The other missionary nurses were getting married, changing ministry or on furlough. It looked like I was the only constant left in the equation. The head nurse's job with all the extra responsibilities was falling to me! And *my* heart was turning to evangelism.

I shared my heart's desires with those over me and they agreed to delegate some of the load. But there was still no solution to the nursing need. I had said goodbye to my Dutch coworker with a teary eyed embrace. Then I was left alone in our three bedroom house with her friendly rich-brown dachshund as my only companion. The prospect of eleven months alone looked like eleven years when there were no peers to share it with me. The Holy Spirit's stream of inner praise was the only thing to keep me from feeling lonely.

One night my doggy friend got violently ill. I had just had the house sprayed with a potent insecticide for ants and roaches. Evidently he had eaten a small house lizard that had succumbed to the poison. I broke down and cried, "Lord, are You going to take even my dog away?" I nursed him through the night with prayer and a teaspoonful of milk every hour. And he recovered to father a healthy litter of adorable little wiener pups.

It was March 1975 and political tensions in Southeast Asia were nearing the breaking point. The unexpected capture of C&MA missionaries Betty Mitchell, Dick and Lillian Phillips, and Norman and Joan Johnson in Banmethuot, Vietnam was followed by a wholesale evacuation of all missionaries from that country. We were stunned! The missionaries in Cambodia and Laos likewise were forced to make surprise exits as their countries too were overrun by communists. In the prominent domino theory of the day, Thailand was next in line to go down the road under communist control.

The American military advised us that our Maranatha campus would be a prime target for insurgents. We had medical facilities, a pure water supply, rice and produce. In fact, the shallow river bordering our rice fields was a scant deterrent to known communist infiltrators already in the village next to us.

The mission drew up evacuation plans for escape by road, boat or helicopter. Even my dog, being a rare breed in Asia, was granted permission for a helicopter flight should our evacuation be necessary. The essentials in our packed emergency suitcases included black shoe polish to put on our faces should we need to disguise our white skin. We knew that if the communists broke across the Mekong River from Laos to Thailand at night they could march to our doorstep by breakfast time. It was a very disquieting thought. There were no government phones to our village and shortwave radios were against the law.

Meanwhile there were personnel problems surfacing among the national staff at the clinic. Disunity among them eventually erupted into the unheard of: our entire Thai clinic staff called a strike, leaving us missionaries emotionally confused and wounded. It was like a slap in the face, and particularly painful to the missionary doctor and nurse who had labored so many years among these Christians. It was one factor that later led to the mission terminating medical ministries.

I was in an emotional upheaval over all that was happening when a missionary colleague dropped in from Khonkaen town. *The Lord bless you and keep you,* she spontaneously sang out in greeting. I knew it was a word from God to me. What a healing balm to soothe my troubled heart!

April 30, 1975 was a never-to-be-forgotten day. It was a Wednesday so the clinic was closed. I had just been to town to care for government work permit business and arrived home at Maranatha shortly before supper. I dumped my passport and papers unceremoniously on the bed and was just stepping out of a cold shower when the wind whipped up. My hair still wet and wrapped in a towel turban style, I struggled to reach between the screens and iron bars to close the flapping wooden window shutters. A recently arrived house mate, a nurse evacuee from Cambodia ran in commanding—"Don't! You'll injure your wrist! Quick, get a flashlight and a blanket and get down to the basement!"

I looked at her blankly—*was she kidding or for real? Why did I need a flashlight? And why a blanket? Basement?* Our Thai style house was on stilts and all we had downstairs were a couple dark storerooms full of empty barrels. What on earth could she mean? As a Floridian she was well acquainted with tornadoes and this had the markings of such.

I felt silly going downstairs and letting rain pour in my windows upstairs. Then as suddenly as it had started it stopped. I was ready to go upstairs again. "No, no," she pleaded. "This is only the eye of the storm. The other side will reach us soon." To my amazement her prediction proved right.

At the doctor's house next door the dining table had been set for supper. The force of the wind left the dishes and silverware in a heap on the floor. A large tree was partially uprooted and damaged the roof over their bedroom. At the clinic outpatient rooms the patients were huddled under the beds. At the Bible School campus the thatch roofs blew off the chicken coops. The hens didn't lay eggs for a week, they were so rattled. In the village, tin roofs and thatch walls had blown around. Miraculously there were no serious injuries. Only the electricity was knocked out for the night. One half hour away in Khonkaen town not a drop of rain had fallen nor had there been a wisp of wind.

Never before had anyone in the area experienced such a storm. Thunder, lightening and typhoons were common, but not a tornado. One villager reported seeing a strange red circle in the sky and said, "Look!" But before her husband could turn around the fiery ball had hit. Our housekeeper and her extended family spent that night camped on our living room floor. The red dust from across the river left mud spots on everything including my passport—a visual evidence and reminder of the event.

The year 1975 saw thousands of refugees pouring onto Thai soil from Vietnam, Cambodia and Laos. The Christian and Missionary Alliance responded by opening a CAMA Services relief office to assist refugees in various camps. The political situation in Thailand itself was still not at all stable. In Maranatha many questions were raised as to the wisdom of the missionaries remaining in such insecure conditions. One missionary family desired to move into town but would not do so if it meant leaving behind the two houses of single ladies (clinic and Bible School staff) were insisting on staying. For myself I felt no urge of the Spirit to move.

Then one night a small grenade was thrown on a major bridge of the main highway between our village and town. It was our main route to safety and the incident caught our attention. The next day God clearly revealed to my spirit – no matter what anyone else did I was to move out! My coworker concurred fully. She'd been nervous for some time about the situation. So that day we drove into town to see a house God had pictured in my mind.

We found it was vacant. We located the owner and discovered that he had *two* appropriate houses for rent.

The decision was made by the mission executive committee to move *all* personnel out of Maranatha. Within three weeks we were packed and moved—yes, into the very house God had indicated to me. We now commuted by Land Rover during daylight hours to work in the clinic and Bible School. It was a drastic change of lifestyle—housekeepers, pets and vehicle schedules had to adjust.

Six weeks later I was in Bangkok for a memorable week. I had been notified that my resident visa to live in Thailand had finally been granted after six years of applying and extending temporary visas. I decided to take advantage of the occasion and prepared a small gift for each of the 200 employees in the immigrations office. I started with the Chief of Immigrations and went to each desk with a Gospel of Mark, Bible booklets and tracts. To each one I said, "In celebration of getting my visa I want to present you this gift." I was well received until I came to a mid level police officer's room.

"How many thousand *baht* did you have to pay?" he queried.

"The normal 200 *baht* fee," I answered.

"No, how many thousand," he persisted. Flustered, I began to pull my receipt out to show him. "You mean you only paid 200 *baht*? The going price is 2,000." He shook his head in disbelief. I explained that we had been praying for it for six years.

There was a second big event that week. The members of the Thai nurse association of which I was a member were to have an audience with her Majesty the Queen of Thailand. As usual the month of October was rainy and many roads were flooded in Bangkok. I was staying at the Alliance Guest Home where they had sand bags at the gate to try to keep out the flood waters. To meet the queen we were expected to wear a floor length formal dress. However for me to reach the main road from the Guest Home to hail a taxi required that I step over the sand bags and wade through murky water mid-calf deep. So I put on my old blue rubber slippers and pulled my long skirt up to my knees, and carried my high heeled shoes in a paper bag. The neighbors on the lane asked where I was going.

"To meet the queen," I replied. I'm sure they thought I was kidding! Once I got to the lecture hall of the prestigious Chulalongkorn University I ducked into a restroom to wash my feet and legs and put on proper shoes. The slippers were left to their fate in a corner.

In spite of a heavy rain the queen kept her appointment with the nurses. We were thrilled to listen to her gracious words and to have the opportunity to see her in person. As we were dismissed after the royal audience, it began to rain again. About 40 of us found shelter in a side room of the auditorium. To our surprise the beloved queen entered the same room to wait out the downpour. Our elegant conversations were no more than a stammered, "How do you do, Your Majesty?" We five or six foreign nurses were obvious among the couple hundred immaculately uniformed Thai nurses. We felt honored.

But the most important event of the week for me was the return of our captured missionaries from Vietnam – Betty Mitchell, the Phillips and Johnsons. C&MA President Dr. Nathan Bailey and Dr. L.L. King flew to Bangkok to welcome them. At the Guest Home we were briefed the night before the expected release, that we could not be entirely sure that the communists would keep their promises to us. If the missionaries really were released, we should not expect them to want to talk. Having been confined to the jungles since their capture eight months earlier their physical and mental states could be altered. We were told they would need time to process their experiences and adapt to civilization again.

Since I had worked in the Dalat School I knew these parents as well as their children. Teenager Gerry Mitchell had been allowed to fly up to Bangkok to meet her mother. As I stood by her side at the Bangkok airport we were all silently praying and holding our breath. Would Gerry's father, Archie Mitchell captured in 1962, be among the released captives? We strained our eyes to see as the passengers deplaned. A tall, thin but straight Betty Mitchell was spotted and red-haired Dick Phillips was identified on the tarmac as they boarded the bus to the terminal building. But no Archie. Embassy officials and cameramen were among those who jammed the VIP room. I couldn't restrain my excitement and thankfulness at seeing the missionaries alive again. As each one stepped off the airport shuttle bus I gave them a big welcome home hug. And then everyone boarded vans to ford the flooded streets of Bangkok to the Alliance Guest Home.

A special easy to digest meal was served that night in anticipation of the shrunken stomachs that had been fed (or not fed) who knows what. There was a long silence and then a deeply emotional moment as a prayer of thanksgiving was made over our supper. Our soup was salted with tears of gratefulness. We could not imagine what our fellow workers had been through on the trails. On the other hand, they were struggling to comprehend that they were finally *free!*

Contrary to our expectations the freed captives were all talking at once. They were relating experiences and asking questions about events during their absence. Betty Mitchell had been very special to me. As a kid in boarding school I remembered her as "Aunt Betty" who had made us taffy for Friday fun nights. After Archie's capture she had been a model of trust to me. Her youngest daughter, Gerry, had been my youngest sister, Melody's roommate when I was school nurse in Penang. It was indeed a special bonus from the Lord to be present for this historic occasion.

The next day I had to return to work at Maranatha—an eight hour bus ride north. As our bus vied for space on the jammed traffic lanes of Bangkok I happened to notice a passenger on another bus to our right. On the front page of his Thai newspaper were two large photos—one of Betty and Gerry Mitchell, and another photo of me hugging Dick Phillips. The caption read "Relatives Greeting Freed Captives." They were right—the missionary family is often closer than blood relatives.

The whole of 1975 had been one big upheaval – emotionally, physically, and spiritually. It was not one I would want to repeat.

At the end of 1975 I wrote my resignation. I could not continue as head nurse of the clinic when God was wooing me into more direct evangelism. As it turned out, the resignation was not necessary. The mission leadership had made the difficult decision to close the clinic. Our doctor had not returned to the field and we could not legally continue without a physician. For some months we had been referring our leprosy patients to government clinics. Both societal attitudes towards people with leprosy, and medical practice had changed. New medicines effectively decimated the micro bacteria to safe levels almost overnight. No longer were patients isolated from society since they weren't contagious. Their months of healing and recovery could be at home with their families.

My coworker, Mabel Hartman had served in Laos previously and spoke Laotian—a language similar to the northeastern Thai dialect. No longer tied to clinic responsibilities we began visiting the village churches in Khonkaen province on Sundays. We decided that if the national church would have to go underground as in Vietnam, Laos and Cambodia it should be prepared. We prayed for four churches to ask us for teaching.

One Sunday we set off for a church that was an hour down the highway and another hour over rutted country roads. We bounced and bumped so hard that twice the Land Rover's spare tire vibrated loose. Mabel was an exhausted driver by the time we reached the church. It was a simple wall-less structure, just a thatched roof shading crude wooden plank benches. Children and animals freely ambled in and out. A young mother came and tied a cloth hammock to a church post and a nearby tree and rocked her infant while participating in the service.

"Never mind," I comforted Mabel. "We'll not come here again." But I was wrong.

The group of Christians that day very eagerly asked us, "Now that the clinic is closed, what are you doing?" We could not lie and admitted that we were teaching in churches. Their immediate response was "Good, you can come and teach here."

We outlined strict conditions. A church must hold its usual Sunday School and worship service. Then we would teach in the afternoon. There would be required homework and scripture memorization. If they didn't do their part we would stop.

That day as I tried to keep the Rover on the road for our homeward journey I apologized to Mabel who was ten years my senior. "I'm sorry, Mabel, I couldn't refuse their enthusiasm. We'll have to write our prayer partners immediately to pray extra hard for the third Sunday of every month when we come out here."

Mabel had songs and memory work to teach. I trained them in inductive Bible study and how to witness. In this church the elders rotated pastoral responsibilities each year. Their preaching was no more than reading a passage of scripture and making a couple of comments. As an incentive to memorize scripture we offered Old Testaments to anyone who committed 85 verses to memory. In this little church no one even owned an Old Testament volume. To our delight, a young mother, a 70 year old man and the presiding elder for the year earned their Old Testaments.

One Sunday the primary prayer request of these church members was for rain. My lesson was on faith. Around the church I could see the pathetic tapioca crop, dry and withering. "Faith requires action to authenticate it," I explained. "Why don't you pray for rain as Elijah did. But you must pray in faith believing God will answer. If you believe He will send rain, get your water jars lined up with the rain spouts from your roof tops." Out of desperation and necessity they took the challenge to heart and prayed then and there. As we gathered up our books and belongings to head home, we did not notice the clouds gathering overhead until suddenly big rain drops began to fall. The rain came so hard and fast that the canvas roof over the back of the Land Rover was little protection for our teaching materials and equipment.

We rejoiced in such an immediate response to prayer. Soon we had to shift into four wheel drive as the fine dust turned to mud. My big thick Thai Bible was so thoroughly drenched it was days before it dried out. In fact, I had to send it to Bangkok to have a new binding put on. Even today its water stained pages remind me of the faith of a little village church who petitioned our Father for their needs.

Khonkaen city was the hub for C&MA work in northeast Thailand. The Central Bible School was in town as was the headquarters for the Gospel Church of Thailand (the Thai counterpart of The Christian and Missionary Alliance). Annual church conferences and all large meetings were accommodated on the Bible School property.

Youth conferences were gaining momentum at this time and the goal was to have the biggest ever youth meeting that year—1977. As one of the mission youth advisors I was heavily involved. A leader, Miss Buakaap, had worked with mass media in Bangkok. She had a strong desire to stage an Easter program on the local TV station. She had a written script and sketches for a backdrop ready. But all her inquiries and requests were met with a negative response. Nevertheless she carried her presentation along to Khonkaen when she came to youth conference.

Four hundred young people came to the campus from over a dozen provinces. It was exciting! On Friday afternoon of the conference Buakaap came to me and said, "Joy, would you drive me over to the TV station. I think they should know about this conference. This is news. Maybe we can get in a word about Easter as well." We prayed together and then went to approach the station manager. In true Thai fashion she was dressed appropriately, spoke politely and had a beautiful smile.

"Wait a minute," the manager said after some conversation. "I happen to have a 30 minute empty slot on Saturday. It was supposed to be a documentary. If you can cook up a program in 19 hours it is yours—free." We were stunned. Did we hear right?

We shifted into high gear. Typists were busy all night preparing three copies of the script which had to be at the station by morning for approval. People at the conference were drafted to practice special music. Costumes were needed. One of my long dresses was a perfect fit for one girl. This feverish activity was in the midst of continuing a full scale youth conference. But God did it. And in nineteen hours the youth watched their own program on the local TV.

It was Easter Sunday and each group of young people wanted a picture taken with the youth advisors. We stood in the hot mid-morning April sun for a dozen or more photos. Then we sat in the big tent for the services, but there was scant relief from the heat. I touched the top of my head and heat seemed to radiate out of my head. By noon I was feeling panicky and desperate to get cool. I drove a missionary colleague to the bus station and then drove home. I drank a big glass of fruit drink and lay down on the cool concrete floor of the living room. My mind was a blur. It wasn't until the next day that I realized I had had a sunstroke.

For years afterwards my life revolved around staying out of the sun. My umbrella was an extension of my hand. I never stepped out of the door without it. The doctor told me that I'd have to wear a hat the rest of my life. A retired missionary wrote to me and urged me to buy a pith helmet as protection from a merciless sun. A prayer partner wrote that she was praying for healing for me. *That's nice*, I thought. I was resigned to live with my handicap of super sensitivity to the sun.

Years later I was challenged by a visiting Dutch pastor's question, "Why put up with it [limitation]?" Suddenly God gave me the faith and I was healed instantly after seven years of avoiding the sun. There was no prayer on my part—just a faithful intercessor praying somewhere in North America.

During this second term on the field I had been given the mission Land Rover to use since no one else needed it. It was aging but still serviceable. One day I experienced God's protection when I turned the wheel to the left but the car went to the right instead. The steering post had come loose. I was on a town street but I hit no one. Three days later I would have been driving on a village road far from any help. I knew God's timing and protection were perfect.

Although Thailand had not succumbed to communist rule there were active insurgents in many northeast provinces. As a mission our policy was to avoid ambush by being off the highways before dark and not to start out before daylight. As an added precaution I never left town without a Thai female companion, often the housekeeper who lived with me.

I was driving a Toyota van going to a village church in the next province one day when I needed a guide. No men were

73

available, but four teenage girls offered their services. Nearing the village we came to a single lane wooden bridge. As usual I took a good look before attempting to cross. It was in disrepair and I could see that the wheels would likely fall into a hole. How were we going to cross?

Then I saw it—a long piece of lumber beside the road. It took two girls to carry it and it was a perfect fit for the hole! I instructed the girls to walk ahead of me in line with the tires so I'd be sure I didn't get too close to the edge. There were no railings on the side of the bridge. To my dismay, half way across I discovered another hole in the bridge.

My tires would fall right in. But God was prepared. The girls lifted the original plank and it fit just as well into the second aperture. I prayed no one would remove it while we were in the village or we'd never get out. This was an area of known heavy insurgency and we dared not leave the main road.

Later we praised God as we exited the village the same way we had gone in. I concluded that an angel must have provided the plank at the side of the road for us. A couple weeks later I received a letter from the missionary colleague in America who had loaned me the vehicle for the year. She asked what happened on a certain day. She had had a heavy burden to pray for my safety. I looked at the calendar and thought, *that's strange— nothing. I was home.* Suddenly I realized she was one day behind us due to the international dateline. That was the day I was crossing the dangerous bridge. God had prompted the owner of the car to pray for my safety!

On another day en route to a leaders' meeting in a neighboring province my companion and I were nearing a bridge. A pickup truck was parked on the shoulder just across the bridge. As usual I slowed down as a precaution lest someone should walk out behind the vehicle without looking. Then it happened. A six year old child darted across the road directly in front of me just as I passed the parked truck. I instinctively slammed on the brakes, turned the steering wheel away and pressed the horn all at once. The van shimmied 100 feet to a stop.

Thoroughly shaken and breathless I suddenly realized there had been no thump or bump of hitting something. I looked in my rear view mirror and saw the child standing in the road looking at me. *I had not hit him after all!* The literature and contents of the van had been tossed and strewn from side to side in the back. Neither my companion nor I had bumped our heads on the windshield. We had not gone over the precipitous edge of the road or hit the oncoming car.

My only explanation was that an angel had intervened, holding the child back with one hand and steering our van with the other. When we arrived at the leaders' meeting half an hour later I was the first one to give a testimony of praise to God for His protection. As a tangible act of thanksgiving I gave an extra large gift in the morning's offering.

Some months later I was in the security of my home in Khonkaen city when I was awakened suddenly at 4 o'clock in the morning. There were two robbers in my bedroom. I thought that I must be dreaming until I saw a flashlight. Then I screamed and pulled a sheet up over my head. "Be quiet!" they ordered, as one of them pointed a gun at me. The presence of the Holy Spirit immediately came over me.

"I'm not afraid of your gun. I have God," I said matter of factly. They rummaged around the dresser. And I could see in the semi-darkness that they had picked up my camera. I had just finished a roll of black and white film for our mission publication and hadn't removed the roll from the camera yet.

"You can have the camera but let me have the film," I bargained. They handed me the camera and I fumbled in the dark to unload it. "Would you shine your flashlight here so I can see what I'm doing?" I requested. They did so. They took the camera and I got the film. Then it was the small cassette recorder they picked up, "You can have the recorder but give me the tape," I asked again. They complied with my request.

"Why are you doing this?" I asked.

"We need money to feed our families. Now where do you keep your money? Where is the man in the house?" they asked. All the while I was praying in tongues under my breath.

"Listen, sit down here on the bed. I have something to tell you," I ordered. They obediently sat beside me in the darkness. [I was decently attired in a cotton night dress.] "Do you know why I've come to Thailand?" I continued "I've come to tell people about Jesus. But if you lie and kill and steal you are going to hell. And not for just ten years or 100 years but forever and ever!"

"Well what should we do?" they asked.

"You have to repent and believe in Jesus," I replied. They grunted and got up. They had heard enough.

One left the room and the other robber turned and said, "Go to bed." I naively thought he was leaving too. But when he threatened rape, I began to panic. Years before when I was a senior in nursing school one of our single C&MA missionary ladies had been raped and murdered in Indonesia. I had cried and prayed, "Lord, what if that happens to me? Can I trust You to protect me from such an experience?" Suddenly that was what was facing me.

I stood there and fought with him. He slapped my cheek. The words of the Lord Jesus came to me and I said, "Jesus said if we are slapped on one cheek to turn the other." So he slapped my other cheek. It didn't hurt, but when he slapped me a third time, I was stunned and thought he might knock me out. I was concerned about what he might do to the two Thai girls sleeping in the other bedrooms. I decided I had better yell for help. I expected he would shoot me, but I knew I was ready to meet the Lord.

I took a deep breath and yelled as loud as I could in Thai, "Help! Robbers! Missionary's house. Call the police!" As I yelled the robber rushed out of my room. He had not touched me inappropriately anywhere. I had sustained only a couple bruises on my neck where he tried to push me down.

My two Thai girlfriends awakened at my yelling. Together we walked through the house room to room to see where the robbers had entered. We discovered that two locks and three bolts on the kitchen door had been cut with heavy tools. The robbers evidently were from a construction site behind us.

As I was yelling for help the next door neighbors were re-turning home from the bar where they worked. They immediately summoned the police. Within minutes police and neighbors with guns came in the house. I told them what happened and again shared the Gospel briefly. There was no way I could describe the intruders since I'd not seen their faces in the dark, but I could smell their sweaty clothing. God had protected us again.

Because the robbers had stolen my wallet with my driver's license, I had to go to the police station to get a temporary driving permit that morning. A news reporter there noticed me and asked what I had come for. I simply answered "a driver's license" and offered nothing more. However, he read the police log and by evening the whole northeast knew of the incident through radio or newspaper. It was reported that the robbers were masked and I had read the Bible to them—neither of which was true!

The next day I was scheduled to drive to a five day ladies' retreat in a village several provinces away. As I traveled the five hours to the meeting I was puzzled why the ladies to be picked up were not at the roadside as prearranged. I had to take time to drive into their villages only to find they had gone to the rice fields. They had heard on the radio about the robbery and surmised I'd not be able to come!

When I finally got to the designated village it was very strange. People seemed to be security conscious. "Missionary, don't park your car there." "Missionary, are the car windows securely locked?"

The last night after the ladies' retreat the village headman and school principal came to the home where I was staying. They talked and asked strange questions late into the night. About midnight I excused myself to crawl under the mosquito net to sleep, since I was the only driver for the long trip home the following day.

The next morning a deaconess said to me, "Don't ever stay in this village again; it's not safe. The headman and principal are communists who censor everything coming in and out."

When I dutifully reported this to our field chairman he exclaimed, "Oh no! I was thinking it was a different village you were going to. I've not stayed in that village for five years. I always go into town and stay at the police barracks." Again God had protected me. Whether in my own home or in a communist village I could trust Him for safety.

Back home again I discovered I was wakeful at night. Every click of the small house lizard's call or the flutter of a stray moth, and I was wide awake, reliving the robbery scene in vivid detail. I knew I needed a healing of those memories and requested prayer for it. Finally one night I sat up in bed and placing my hands on my own head I said, "Lord, I claim healing of my memories." And that was it—He healed me and I had no more problem sleeping.

God had protected me. I could trust Him with my safety on the road or at home. I could trust him to heal my body and my mind. His Word proved true many times over.

11—Potato Soup and a Bushel of Garlic

"Why don't you dye your hair black? You look just like an American!" The village lady was weaving Thai silk on her loom as she eyed me.

"Well, I *am* an American," I objected. "Both my father and my mother are 100% Americans." In a post-Vietnam war era I was assumed to be a half breed whose looks favored my American father more than my assumed Asian mother. Having spoken Thai as a child I had very little accent to suggest I was anything but Thai! I was dressed village style in a wrap around Thai skirt and simple blouse. My five foot stature only added to their assumption that I wasn't truly an American.

As was often the case, there were not enough missionaries to cover all the mission stations. Frequently the missionary couple in an adjacent province would be assigned to supervise the churches in the absence of a furloughing family. It had been that way for as long as I could remember. The Heckendorfs (who were well known for prodigious and varied ministry feats) were due for furlough. I was living in Khonkaen town and thus was assigned to oversee 30 churches and groups in the two neighboring provinces. I would have to do as best I could with such a huge responsibility.

My colleague had done well to organize leaders' meetings once a month in each province and then visit churches and groups as possible. There was little chance for him to give me an orientation. I was given specific instructions about where to pick up one Thai leader who would then direct me to the next leader, and thereby give as many as possible a ride to the leaders' meeting. "And don't forget to stop for the blind man under the tree," he added.

"Which blind man, which tree, George?" I queried. I soon got the hang of it.

All the leaders were men and expected that I, as the missionary, would do just as my male predecessor had done—preach at each leaders' meeting and preach every time I appeared in their church–expected or unannounced. This was missionary culture. I was not comfortable wearing those shoes. From the start I informed them I would not and could not preach. I would be happy to teach at the monthly leaders' meeting, but one of them would need to be prepared to preach each time. They readily agreed and were pleased with the opportunity.

I decided I would teach Old Testament stories since their knowledge was sketchy at best. I had a hidden agenda. Very few of them owned an Old Testament or had ever read it. Only one leader was a Bible School graduate from the four year program taught at fourth grade reading level. The rest were elders with little or no Bible training at all. And 90% of the leaders were leprous Christians. By teaching from the Old Testament I could whet their appetite to read it for themselves. Driving a Land Rover at that time, I could easily carry a supply of Old Testaments to use at the meetings. It wasn't long before they were buying them from me. My mission was accomplished.

As long as I had a Land Rover to use I could navigate the country roads without too much difficulty. Often, seeing a mud hole or a wide stream ahead, I would have to get out of the car and manually turn the front wheel knobs to four-wheel drive and chug through the mire, only to get out and turn the knob back to normal once we had conquered the obstacle.

About 95% of the rural people were non-drivers at that time. I sometimes found that their driving directions got me into a tight spot. One time I was repeatedly assured by several men that a particular short cut to the next village was drivable. They knew of trucks that had gone that way. Ignoring my inner doubts I set out with several guides. Soon my worst fears were realized. Holes two feet deep, ruts and boulders faced me. A tanker would have had a rough time of it. "But, Ma'am you can go this way," I was told. Only a bicycle could have negotiated the path around the tree stumps and ditches. There was no going on. Finally I had to back up and take the long way around to the village. Upon arrival I was told. "Yes, trucks did go that route five years ago!"

About this time I invited my Thai housekeeper to live with me in the spacious house I was assigned to, and began mentoring her. She loved to read. I assigned her to read every new Thai book that came from the Christian publishers. Then over our meals she would give me an animated report on the book. Driving out of the city for ministry I always had a female companion and she was usually the one to go with me. I outlined a division of labor. I would teach her the children's lesson and she would teach it to the village kids while I taught the adults. I would schedule the ministries, drive the vehicle and pay the bills. She would keep house, plan menus and teach kids. The first time we returned home bone weary from a country trip, she flopped on the couch to rest. I went to the kitchen and fixed us some lunch. Then I called her to eat. She was so chagrined that I, as her employer and senior, should serve her that she never did it again. We both worked and then both rested. She was intrigued that I could take leftovers and make something new from them. "How do you do it?" she asked.

"I just mix things that taste good together," I answered. I challenged her to experiment. Some meals later I was served potato soup with spaghetti noodles in it. I chuckled remembering that we had had mashed potatoes left over a couple days ago and noodles left over from a previous meal. A week later we had it again. This time I *knew* the ingredients were not leftovers. She had liked it so much she'd made it fresh for us!

When I heard that a Thai evangelist and his son were touring the northeastern provinces and showing Christian movies, I asked them to help me in several villages. The schedule was set and prayer partners in America prepared the way with intercession. By day our team went house to house in a village giving out tracts and the Gospel of John. We witnessed and invited people to the Christian movie in the evening.

At night we erected a large screen under the stars and played music over the speaker system using a small generator. Our team of eight moved prayerfully among the crowds answering questions and observing. At the end of the film the gifted evangelist preached in the northeastern dialect. He kept his listeners' attention for another hour. As a result 19 adults and two children accepted Christ in the 19 day effort.

The villages we had selected were places where a Christian had been active in his or her witness. After three to five nights, we were off to another site. One night a young man in his early 20's approached me to ask, "Could I believe in Buddha and God at the same time?" Before I could answer, the Buddhist amulet around his neck unexplainably broke and fell to the ground. He was so shaken he needed no further answer.

The village of Kampia was less than an hour from the town of Khonkaen where I had made my headquarters. Kampia seemed more receptive to the Gospel than our other sites. Six new people accepted Christ during our meetings with the evangelist. Together with the Christian rice farmer and his wife, there were eight adults. Overnight we had an infant church to nurture. Losing no time, we promised to return on Sunday and hold a service. The Kampia Church was born.

On Sundays my helper gathered the children under the big shady tamarind tree for a story and songs while I taught the adults on the lower level of a nearby house. All village homes were built up on stilts so pigs and buffaloes could be penned underneath. A low bamboo bench or bed to relax on in the shade was where the family napped in the heat of the day or neighbors stopped by to chat.

It wasn't long before the group grew and purchased the lumber from a disassembled old mission home. Teak wood was commonly used for homes and was especially durable. A 12 by 30 foot concrete floor was poured. Slatted wood walls and a tin roof completed the tiny church. It was a striking landmark as one approached the village…Buddhist temple, rice fields, and then a brown wooden Christian church with its cross on the rooftop.

At Christmas time a big celebration was held there in Kampia. To accommodate the crowd for the special event, we met outside the little church. Missionaries George and Edna Heckendorf joined us. As they harmonized an appropriate duet, chickens, dogs and cats ambled in and out of the crowd as unobtrusively as usual. Just as the missionaries sang "the cattle are lowing…" a stray cow meandered in front of them! Only we Americans were amused. The local people found it too commonplace to even notice!

The proximity of Kampia village to the town of Khonkaen made this a favorite visitor site. Guests from overseas wanting to see a real Thai village could observe silk worms eating their way through mountains of mulberry leaves spread on great flat woven bamboo trays. The whole process from seeing the silk threads removed from the cocoons to weaving the famous Thai silk was a normal sight. The village blacksmith with his hand bellows performed obligingly for many a guest. His sweat provoking job was picturesquely framed under a large shade tree at the far end of the village.

Basket weavers sat comfortably in their thatch roofed homes or on the soft ground. A well worn dust covered radio usually prattled nearby as their companion. Always we were welcomed and offered a seat on the grass mat. The host would quickly bring a tin dipper of rain water and invite us to drink. It was bottom line Thai courtesy. In later years Coca Cola could be secured from a nearby neighbor's store. Without electricity in the village the beverage was a warm fizz.

A couple of oddities of nature cropped up in this village as well. I remember when the Christian farmer's sow died suddenly leaving five little suckling piglets orphaned. The farmer was devastated as this was his savings account gone bankrupt! He poured out his heart to his Creator and was pleased and surprised with the forthcoming answer. His mongrel dog had delivered a litter of puppies about the same time as the sow gave birth. When the dog happened to walk in the vicinity of the orphaned piglets it was attacked by them. It seemed that the smell of milk was like a magnet drawing them to a surrogate mother! They would latch on to her and nurse her dry each time. The farmer was delighted. Dogs were considered of no value but pigs were money. One would be sacrificed for the other. So the little pigs were salvaged by powdered milk and nurtured by the dog. The town reporter came to the village and ran the story noting that the pigs had not yet started barking.

The other oddity was a family of chickens whose feathers grew upside down—giving them the appearance of having continuously ruffled feathers. Of necessity they had to scramble for cover at the slightest sprinkle of rain as the upturned feathers collected moisture.

A final adventure in the Kampia village was often a ride in a two wheeled pony cart across the red dirt road to the next village where we would visit an elderly Christian couple.

Theological Education by Extension (TEE) came into popular use in northeast Thailand at this time. I was one of three missionaries to participate. Thai church leaders would complete a five day crash study of a ten week course book with the master teacher. Jiem Meng was a former leprosy patient who became a gifted pastor and teacher. We were oblivious to his gnarled hands, sunken nose, misshapen face and drooping eye as his poignant comments led us through the discussions.

Four of the five courses were translations from English. The exception was the *Basic Doctrines* course. Teacher Jiem Meng himself was the author. It was five times harder than any other course! Never having studied theology in English, I thought I would fail the course. I had come to the mission field as a nurse with only two years of Bible college. I was unfamiliar with the material and the Thai vocabulary stretched my abilities.

After having taken a TEE course, we were expected to go out and for the next ten weeks teach others who would again teach others. I loved the method and material, and had tremendous job satisfaction. Each course required that the student pay 20 *baht* (less than a dollar) in cash or in kind for his book. In one church a poverty stricken elderly man and his wife walked an hour in the hot sun from a neighboring village to come to church services. He wanted to learn TEE even though he could barely manage to read, and could not write. I agreed, and he paid for his book with a *big* bushel of garlic from his field. I had a year's supply of garlic for me and all my friends! He came to class on Sunday afternoon with his book well worn and dog eared—he had read it in the fields as he tended his buffalo! He always gave the right answer when I asked him a question in class--that is, as long as the answer to my question would be "God"!

I had promised myself that I would not offer to teach the difficult doctrine course. I had hardly passed it myself. Surely I could not manage to teach it! But it was unavoidable. An elder in another church with twenty teenagers requested that I teach them that very course. It was a challenge to teach that the first time around. I was teaching high schoolers who could pronounce the words and explain them better than I, their teacher! No doubt their compulsory study of Buddhism in school had whetted their desire to compare the biblical doctrines. More than half the class had perfect attendance and good grades. Years later a pastor and two pastor's wives reminded me they had been young people in that class and were so thankful for the foundation it gave them in their faith. God had touched them in spite of my inadequacies. Twenty years later, it had become one of my favorite courses to teach.

12—A Hundred Chauffeurs

There came a time when there was no mission vehicle available for me to use. I reasoned that the Thai had to use public transportation, and if they could manage without a private car, so could I. It was a decision I never regretted. A whole new life style opened up to me. I found I no longer had to transport books, sacks of rice, chickens and people around to every village every time I went somewhere. I no longer spent time keeping a mission car account and maintaining an aging vehicle. I did not have to arrange for a female companion to accompany me. I had a hundred chauffeurs to choose from—the local bus drivers.

Now I could relax and enjoy the bus ride—with the chickens and crying babies. There were endless opportunities for me to witness to fellow passengers. Khonkaen city where I was living was the hub of bus travel for all of northeastern Thailand. I could go in any direction by bus to one of the 17 provinces.

The bus driver's job was to keep his vehicle on the road and attempt to more or less meet a time schedule. The number of bus seats had nothing to do with how many passengers would be permitted or even coaxed onto the bus. More people meant more revenue for the bus company. It was a rare person who complained that he had to stand for four hours on the jerking bouncing bus. The bus fare was always the same whether you had a whole seat, half a seat, a hot seat (over the bus motor) or no seat at all! People were only too thankful to have wheels under their feet to get them to their destination.

On the other hand the driver's helper never had a spare moment. He jumped on and off the bus at every stop—shoving people's belongings into an already chock full under-carriage luggage compartment. Or he was climbing on the roof to secure baskets of fresh garden produce—tomatoes, cabbage or greens. As a last alternative some dilapidated cardboard boxes could be roped to the back bumper of the bus. He then collected the fares from newly boarded customers and wiggled his way through the aisle crammed with standing passengers to the front of the bus. There he sang out a running commentary to the driver—"Motorcycle on the left…..Buffalo coming up on the right…..Right lane is vacant; pass the bus ahead……Oncoming truck on right…..Bicycle on left…..Stop at the tree ahead for passengers to board…..Stop at the red roofed hut for passengers getting off."

Periodically when the bus was stopped at a long traffic light or in a bus station the driver's helper took a wooden bat-like stick and walloped each tire. The sound emitted revealed to his experienced ear whether or not a tire was getting soft and needed more air. At the end of the day's route it was his job to sweep out the accumulated litter from between the seats and wipe down the bus interior. Then using a battered tin bucket with water and detergent he would wash the outside of the bus by hand. Finally he could bathe and wash his own clothes. Often times these were draped or hung around inside the bus where he slept on the seats for the night.

Traveling by public transportation had its share of surprises. One day a bus I was riding on began to smell of something burning shortly after we left the bus station. After checking around the passenger seats the driver's helper lifted the engine hood. To his chagrin he found that he had forgotten his freshly washed jeans drying on the motor!

Another day I noticed our bus hardly stopping to pick up passengers—an unusual phenomenon in a country where a bus will wait five or six minutes for a villager walking to the highway to board. Then I realized what the helper was yelling to prospective passengers, "Hurry and jump on! The bus brakes can't stop." Understandably I felt uneasy about continuing on this vehicle. When we stopped on an incline the driver's helper threw blocks of wood behind the wheels. I jumped off to wait for the next bus. I preferred a bus with functioning brakes.

Another time a heavily loaded bus I was riding stopped every few miles. The radiator leaked so badly the driver would stop and get a can of water from a pond or stream and pour it in while the helper kept his foot on the clutch. Then we came to a well where several ladies were modestly bathing Thai style with wrap around skirts covering them from their armpits to their knees. Upon request of the driver they laughingly provided us with a pail of water

Late one afternoon as I was riding a bus home there were so few passengers left that the driver decided it wasn't worth continuing the trip. I still had 45 minutes travel to my destination but he stopped and told us he was going no further. The helper would arrange our continuing transportation he said. I thought, *Now what? This has never happened to me before.* Within about ten minutes the helper hailed a passing ten-wheeled truck hauling burlap sacks of rice to the mill. The driver was paid to take five of us into Khonkaen town. We were all crammed onto the single wooden plank seat with the driver. A man with his fighting cock in his arms was seated next to me. When I worried out loud that it would mess on me, he promptly got out and sat on what was left of the wooden plank to right of the driver! (Steering wheels are on the right side because driving is on the left side of the road in Thailand.) It was getting dark as we passed one small town. A policeman was standing in the middle of the road. The driver slowed down and handed him a small banknote without any exchange of words. "What was that for?" I asked.

"I'm overloaded," the driver answered. "The rice bags are higher than the cab's roof. This policeman is easy to pay off." I was sorry I had asked. I felt even less safe a few miles down the road where an overturned gasoline truck blocked three-quarters of the road, and we had to slowly bypass the obstacle by driving on the shoulder. As we tottered momentarily, I prayed desperately that we wouldn't roll over too. Recent stories of kidnappings, rapes and murders came to my mind. I wondered how much I could trust this truck driver. So I started sharing the Gospel with the driver more with a motive of diverting his mind from any thoughts of foul play, than a concern for his spiritual destiny! It was 7 o'clock in the evening when we reached the edge of Khonkaen town safely. I thanked God for protecting me through the various dangers that day.

Another trip I was on an air conditioned tour bus from Bangkok to Khonkaen. En route I was quite amazed to observe a deft change of drivers. We were on a slight down slope on the busy highway traveling probably 50 miles an hour. The driver stood up in his seat, keeping his hands and feet in control of the bus while the relief driver slipped under him into the seat and smoothly took over the controls. The changeover was completed without ever stopping. Obviously this was not the first time they had tried this feat. I couldn't believe my eyes. A bit later I saw the newspaper delivery van driving side by side with us at the same speed. An employee stretched his arm out the passenger window to hand our bus driver the morning's newspaper—delivery at 50 miles an hour! How amazing were my chauffeurs!

Before we closed our mission clinic at Maranatha we had been visited by a young Christian ethnic Chinese doctor and his wife from a neighboring province. He was setting up a private practice in his own home town. He wanted very much to have some help from American nurses such as myself. I had to make a decision. Would I slip back into medical ministries again or would I stick with regular church ministries? Would I give injections or would I continue with spiritual ministry? No, I was enjoying personal evangelism too much to return to full time medical work.

This man was a very innovative physician. From a one room clinic next to the open air fresh market he soon moved into a two story shop house, making it into patient rooms and an operating room. Finding commercial equipment too expensive, he hired a Vietnamese metal worker to fashion an operating table with a hydraulic car jack. An operating room lamp was produced from a discarded American shell casing and a theater spotlight. They proved functional enough. When an x-ray salesman came along, the doctor's wife, an accountant, learned how to run the machine. She was also her husband's right hand during surgery in the operating room.

One time a patient needed a blood transfusion. The doctor's blood was the only match he could find. So he had his wife put the needle into his own arm as he lay on the bed. To facilitate gravity flow the patient lay on the floor to receive a direct blood transfusion from his own doctor. With one exception, he had trained all his own nurses. Who were his patients? A large percentage was undercover communists who wouldn't go to the government hospital in town. They feared being found out. The doctor was willing to take risks and set aside normal medical ethics to assist his own countrymen [regardless of their political stances]. It was all the more reason I felt I had to stick with spiritual ministries. If I were to capitulate and give one injection it would be difficult to refuse the next time I was asked to help. I could do what he couldn't do so well—share the Gospel.

At the doctor's invitation I went as often as I could to his town to be chaplain at his mini-hospital. I would go from room to room giving out Gospel tracts and making friendly conversation. "Have you ever heard of Jesus? No? Where are you from, what district?" Asking what district their home was in virtually told me if they were in communist territory. Everyone knew the mountainous area was a pocket of rebel activity. Of course I didn't let on that I had any such knowledge. I was a 'safe' person because I was an outsider.

A couple of hours after distributing the literature I would make a second round to see which patients or relatives had read the tracts. If there were any interest, I had an immediate open door to share the Gospel. Patients going home were urged to take Christian literature along and share it in their villages. I knew missionaries could not go to the communist areas and the Thai Christians feared to go. Thus the Gospel was sent by the unlikely means of non Christian patients.

In the evenings the doctor would gather patients and their relatives on the big back porch of his house and clinic and say, "I'm a Christian and it's a good way. Ma'am Joy will tell you all about it." The high esteem afforded a medical doctor in rural society ensured that his stamp of approval on Christianity would give me a hearing. One evening before I began I counted 25 men who were from those closed districts. God was making a way for hungry hearts to hear the Gospel.

Another evening in a patient's room I met a young girl who was caring for her mother. I sensed an immediate spiritual interest since she had heard the Gospel previously. She accepted Christ that night. Because it was already late I told her I'd explain more in the morning. To my dismay she was gone by daybreak. Her mother had died during the night leaving her an orphan. It was several weeks before I could locate her in the town. When I *did* find her I began discipling her and she grew rapidly in spiritual things. She studied all five TEE books and attended church regularly. Later she went on to Bible School, then returned and pastored the local church for a time.

One day coming into the doctor's town at sunset I was alarmed to find soldiers every few feet along the streets. I asked the doctor what was going on. He was very nervous and said "You can't stay at my house tonight. It is not safe. Go stay in the hotel and don't leave your room all night no matter what you hear. We are under curfew from 9 p.m. until morning. There's been word that the communists are coming tonight to burn down the provincial buildings. All the important records and documents have been removed to safety in Khonkaen."

Checking into a local hotel with my Thai female companion that night I could *feel* the tension. Wealthy people had brought their most precious belongings and were holed up in the hotel. It was very frightening. There had been attacks on villages in this province already and yet everything had been kept out of the press. I had no idea of any problem, nor did the common people in the next province. All night my Thai helper and I tried to sleep and read scripture together. When morning came we left town. The attack had been averted when the communists learned of the government forces moving in to defend the town.

Besides the hospital ministry I networked with a couple of young men of another denomination who were sent from Bangkok to start a church in the town. As a new Christian the doctor was oblivious to denominations. At that time the various mission organizations had a gentlemen's agreement to stay in certain prescribed areas so as not to overlap our efforts. It made sense— non-Christians could not understand denominational differences. Whenever they asked I tried to explain that Christian denominations were like brands of bread. You could choose wheat bread or raisin bread or whatever, but the basic ingredients were the same. "Don't worry about it—the important thing is to know Jesus personally." In a country that was more than 99% non-Christian there was plenty of work for everyone. There was no sense trying to work in the same places—we needed to spread out and cover the land.

So it was a bit awkward at first when we discovered the doctor had invited both missions to his doorstep. For many years our mission had not been able to place a missionary in residence in this province but we still visited the old Christians who were there. The two young men were new blood—an impetus for a fresh start. The mainstay of the church in the town was a woman who faithfully prayed for her husband for 17 years. It was a day of great rejoicing when he finally accepted Christ. The church woman was the motherly type and looked after the Christian workers well.

I personally had another appreciation for this woman—she was a granny masseuse. Whether driving a Land Rover or bouncing around in creaky old buses I often found myself tensed up and suffering a headache. With no hot shower or tub to soak in I found another cure. This lady knew just how to relax my tense muscles by walking on my back. She was only the first of a number of portly women to introduce me to traditional Thai massage by walking on my back!

Of the many trips I made to this province I invariably sensed a spiritual coldness or blockage as I crossed the border from the neighboring province. Boarding a bus I would give out Gospel tracts while we waited for departure time. But I noticed a difference on these buses. Usually if I offered a tract, "Free literature, good news" most people readily accepted it. However, I found that if the first person refused it, no one else would accept a tract either. Then an idea came to me. The next time someone refused a tract I apologized loudly enough for other passengers nearby to hear. "Oh, I'm sorry. I didn't know you couldn't read. Maybe your nephew or grandchild can read it to you." I never had a problem with someone taking a tract from me after that.

It was October 1978 and the rains had been quite heavy. The water level in the reservoir behind the big dam was nearly a yard higher than was considered safe. Since more rain was expected, the government authorities decided to release some water or the dam could burst and cause a serious flood over several provinces.

I left Khonkaen on a Saturday morning on a bus to go to a leaders' meeting an hour away in the next province. I noticed that one half inch of water was already trickling over parts of the road, and people were evacuating their homes and camping on higher ground—the highway! Several hours later when I returned on the same route it was no longer open to traffic and I had to walk a couple miles in ankle deep water to get home. By nightfall the following day the water was waist deep over the highway and huge chunks of asphalt were breaking away in the swirling current. We heard that a five mile stretch of flooded road was engulfed in a strong current that whisked several people away to their deaths. 120,000 people in the city fled to the Khonkaen University hilltop. The town became a virtual island with flood waters cutting off all roads in and out of the city. The railroad was under water. Rice mills were under water. Three hundred pound water buffaloes were washed away. Rice and fuel had to be flown in from elsewhere for emergency needs.

In the midst of this upheaval my Thai companion and I heard that a Christian widow was crying because her home on stilts was flooding. We hurried to the edge of town to see her but were quite unprepared for what we found. We had to wade into the lane in murky water up to our knees and then midway we got a ride in a small dugout to her house. The waves of the flood water were lapping near the top of her ladder when we arrived. We prayed, we sang and we comforted her from Isaiah 43:1-3: "...When you pass through the waters, I will be with you; and when you pass through the rivers, they will not sweep over you...."

Just then the governor's order came over the radio for everyone to evacuate that area. The water was rising one inch an hour and they feared the dam would break. The dugout we had arrived in was suddenly drafted to transport people's belongings, so we humans had no choice but to clamber down the ladder and into the filthy water. I was wearing a dress and I had to wade in the rising waist deep muddy water. (I was well aware that the pigs' pen and buffalo stall had been under the house-on-stilts.) There were snakes and blood suckers to watch for also. When I finally got home that day I scrubbed and soaked my clothes in strong disinfectant several times. Eventually the odor and mud color came out of my clothing.

Providentially my vacation was scheduled to start that week. But I wondered if I could get out of the city of Khonkaen. The provincial buses still ran to the edge of town. And we were told that a lightweight pickup truck would then take us across the bridge. Instead we were dumped off near the bridge. The police were now stopping all traffic as three bridges had already collapsed in the swirling murky waters. We were instructed to pile onto a waiting flat bottomed boat. Not being a swimmer, I was thoroughly frightened. The boat was overloaded and had to be maneuvered around treetops, roofs and electric lines. To my great relief several miles down the road we stepped out of the boat and walked another mile to a waiting bus. The usual seven hour trip to Bangkok stretched to eleven hours with numerous detours necessitated by other flooded areas. I vowed I would not return to my mission station until the trains or buses could go all the way. One scary boat trip was enough!

A month later when I did return the worst flood in northeast Thailand in 60 years was over. The countryside was a pathetic mess. The light green rice seedlings which had graced the paddy fields were dry brown wisps of straw clinging to fences, tree branches and in some places, electric lines where flood waters had deposited them. God had been with me when I passed through the waters. They did not overflow me!

13—Another Call

My second furlough, the summer of 1979, was anticipated with a shadow of sadness. Before arriving in America my paternal grandmother for whom I was named, went to be with the Lord. I had been away for four years and now I'd missed seeing her by just two months. I comforted myself that no doubt she could see me from heaven's heights. Although I didn't know it then, it was part of the price I was paying to serve the Lord overseas. I was not present for even one of my four grandparents' funerals. I had already missed two sisters' weddings and would miss my brother's in the future as well. But the weekly detailed family letters helped to fill the loss I felt.

This furlough was filled with many of those special family occasions, as if to make up for lost time. My sister Faith had regularly sent me photos of her two children. But my first real glimpse of this niece and nephew were when I arrived home. The children were already four and one half and three years of age. They each approached me rather hesitantly with grubby little fistfuls of wilting golden dandelions for "Auntie Joy."

The last week of May was highlighted by my sister Carol and her husband graduating from Simpson College in San Francisco. That very night she gave birth to her first child. Since her labor was short and both Mother and I (a midwife) were staying with them in their mobile home, my sister came home from the hospital only 12 hours after delivery. So I had the joy of helping care for her and my not yet day-old niece.

Four days later my brother Tim graduated from Golden Gate Seminary, also in the Oakland Bay area. Then my youngest sister, Melody, purposely chose her wedding date around my ministry schedule so I could be the maid of honor. It was a joyous occasion for all 14 of us, including Grandpa Boese, to be together.

My fall and spring speaking tours covered Hawaii, California, Arizona and New Mexico. The Hawaiians lived up to their reputation of gracious hospitality. I was greeted with fragrant flower leis and orchid corsages of every description every time I turned around. But I unexpectedly experienced several days of culture shock my first few days there. I was comfortable in Thai society and equally at ease in California's culture. But Hawaii seemed to be a mix of oriental and western cultures. In many homes removing one's shoes before entering the home was the norm as it was in Thailand. However, my automatic reaction for greeting someone was the Thai two hands together greeting—not shaking hands as an American!

I couldn't help staring at the blonde haired fellows and girls pedaling three wheeled pedicabs for hire along Waikiki Beach. We had exactly the same kind of pedicabs in Asia but only black haired men engaged in this lowliest of employments. I felt ill at ease to know whether to respond as in Asia or in America!

Soon it was time to think about packing for my return to Thailand again. In 50 weeks I had taken over 260 speaking engagements. This was due, in part, to having 30 C&MA churches within an hour's drive of my parents' home there in southern California. I had been loaned a brand new 1979 Dodge Colt to use for the year and made good use of it to go everywhere possible. It was no wonder I returned to the field exhausted. (On subsequent furloughs I learned to set times for holidays and to limit speaking engagements to three times per week outside of the regular tours.)

I arrived back in Bangkok unsure of what to expect for my third term. Ordinarily every missionary is given an assignment ahead of time, but a communications lapse had left me clueless. I knew only that I was to be in Thailand. When I contacted the field chairman a few days after arriving he was aghast when I asked about my assignment. Had no one told me? I was expected immediately in Khonkaen to cover the Bible School administration for three or four months while George and Edna Heckendorf took a short furlough. They were leaving their post within 24 hours. What a surprise to me!

I arrived at the Khonkaen train station at 10 a.m. and was met by a Thai Bible School teacher. Twelve hours later I was waving goodbye to the Heckendorfs! The hours between were one big blur of instructions and hasty directions. I followed George around all day with pen and paper jotting down notes and signing on to a bank account for the Bible School. After the send off, I returned to their house alone that night, my mind in a whirl. In which one of the bedrooms were my suitcases? I had not even seen them since I arrived in the morning. How did I lock up the house—chains, padlocks and bolts?

The Heckendorfs had offered me the use of the only air conditioned bedroom in the house—the master bedroom. It had a king sized water bed in it. Since the telephone was also in that room I thought I would try sleeping on the water mattress for a new experience. However, I soon found that if I slept in the middle of the bed I couldn't slosh my way over to the phone in time. So I slept on one side for a week and then on the other side for a week and changed the sheets every two weeks. It was marvelous. Since it was the first waterbed in northeast Thailand I made it a tourist attraction for my Thai visitors. The concept of sleeping on a water mattress triggered a number of questions. "Don't you get wet?.....Isn't it cold?.....Why aren't you electrocuted by the warming mechanism?"

The Heckendorf house gave me my exercise answering the two back porch door buzzers, a front door, a campus intercom and telephone. I had to constantly run from one to the other. My nursing triage training was put to good use—which buzzer or ring was most urgent and which could be delayed momentarily?

At the Bible School were a newly completed four story dormitory, gymnasium and four unit staff housing. Hundreds of keys for all the various doors were unsorted in a box. We were still working out problems with sewer pipes and the water pump. It seemed that every day I needed to have an hour's phone consultation or write a three page letter to George. "What do I do about this?.....Where's the key for the storeroom kept?.....Mr. U came to get money for the chicken coops. What's that deal about?.....The construction foreman says he forgot to put in air vent pipes in the apartment cesspool tanks. He will need extra money to dig up the ground out back. Where do I get money for that?"

I could see why no one else would agree to fill such a mammoth octopus of a job! Furthermore, I had not realized that I'd have to pray in the finances also!

One warm payday morning the Bible school dean asked if we had enough money for the payroll. When I checked the accounts I found we had insufficient funds. After a busy morning I lay down for an afternoon siesta and prayer session. Just then the phone rang. It was a campus room renter saying he wanted to pay in advance as he would be away for the month. By late afternoon enough students had made payments on their fees that I was able to issue the staff and faculty payroll. God had been faithful to the moment!

The rainy season was beginning and with it, I discovered more problems. The missionary home was evidently a pre-World War II edifice. The concrete roof tiles had long ago out-lived their warranty. One rainy evening I came to the back porch to answer a doorbell and found little streams of water everywhere—on the ironing board, on the tables, and on the chairs. I began counting and quit after identifying 70 leaks! Having no access to house repair funds, I decided to phone the field chairman for advice and emergency funding. Eventually the house was to be torn down, but in the meantime it needed to be habitable.

It seemed that everything I was totally ignorant of or in-adequate to deal with was tossed in my lap those months. My only consolation was that there was an end in sight. I was just a stop-gap answer for a never-ending job. It was with great relief that I turned the keys back to the director and his wife after three months. It was field conference time and now I would receive my assignment for the term. But a most uncharacteristic decision was made. I was to make my own choice what I would do among half a dozen needs and ministries.

Providentially I had a couple weeks of vacation scheduled at the beach. After a very hectic furlough and no less demanding stint at the Bible School, I needed a rest. As I spent time alone with the Lord I became strongly impressed that He was calling me in a new direction.

I had always had an affinity for prayer. I had read every-thing I could on the subject. For years before and in the future I always found a prayer group. Sometimes it was one woman, but maybe it would be three or four who shared my burden to pray on a regular basis. At times it would be a daily prayer time at six a.m. when we would meet for an hour. Other times it was at a church with a larger group for three days a week. But this was different. It was a call to be an intercessor.

My concept of an intercessor was like Rees Howells or John Hyde in yesteryears, who spent long hours on their knees. It was retired women like C&MA missionary Marthena Ransom of India, who sat in rocking chairs and prayed through long lists. *But, Lord, that's for the people at home,* I objected. *I'm only 35. I'm not old yet. I'm strong and healthy. I'm not crippled and infirm. Why I'm the missionary! They are supposed to be praying for me.*

But the knowledge of the calling was sure. As definite as my salvation was to me and as clear as my call to be a missionary, I knew God was calling me to be an intercessor. I knew it was useless to resist—I'd been called. I felt if I didn't obey I might end up with some incapacitating disease that would leave me bedridden and unable to do anything *but* pray. *"Okay, Lord. But You are going to have to teach me how to be an intercessor,"* I bargained. *"All the intercessors I know are in America. You'll have to make the mission agree—to have me sit around and pray. Will the mission board even allow it? Missionaries are sent out to work and be active."*

I was at peace, a bit excited and not a little curious where the road ahead would lead. I didn't have any models on the field, but I knew that He who called me obviously would guide. I was not to worry, nor did I have long to wait.

14—"Usha"

Passing through Bangkok en route back to Khonkaen I heard a bizarre story. A Swiss missionary refugee worker visiting the town of Ubon was asked by her Thai Christian companion, "Why is it that westerners are going into Buddhism? We Thai are leaving Buddhism to become Christians. There is a German girl living in a forest monastery as a Buddhist nun. Won't you go talk to her?" Together they traveled out of the town to find her. It was God's time. The missionary led the German woman to Christ. What a fantastic story, *but* the girl was still residing in the temple grounds.

For nearly 30 years she had wandered through shallow Christianity, cults, Hinduism and now Buddhism. Searching for peace of heart and mind, she was impelled and empowered by demonic spirits. As an infant she had been christened in the state church as "Ursula." Wandering the hills of the Himalayas in India, searching for her guru, she was given the name "Usha." Finding no answers, she came to Thailand—the land of Buddhism. It was an attempt to fill her vacant heart.

The Buddhist temple she entered was a forest monastery, well known among world travelers who were seeking answers. "Why do I exist? Is there a god?" She shaved her head and donned the white robes of a Buddhist nun. She began to study meditation under the temple's famous founder and head abbot. She lived in a simple wooden dwelling called a kuti among the trees of the forest.

Usha applied herself to the discipline with avid sincerity. There were eight precepts for nuns: Refrain from killing any living thing—even a worm or a mosquito (because when people die and are reincarnated according to their good and bad deeds, the insect could be your reincarnated relative). Refrain from stealing, lying, or desiring another's spouse. Refrain from intoxicants of all kinds. Refrain from amusements and luxuries. Sleep humbly and lowly no higher than a cubit from the ground or floor. Eat only one meal a day--before noon.

For months Usha meditated on her breath as she inhaled and exhaled. She wore a path among the dry leaves of the forest with her 18 measured paces required for walking meditation. Living within the brick walls and iron gates, she was seemingly in semi-confinement. She failed to see the contradiction of her actions. She filtered every drop of drinking water through a cloth strainer to keep from taking the life of even the most minute insect, but she easily swallowed pieces of buffalo meat with her meals. She took caution not to step on a wandering ant or beetle, but preserved the wooden house posts with anti-termite poison. She arose at 3 a.m. on Buddhist holy days to chant sacred words. When she was burning with fever, writhing in pain or doubled in discomfort of tropical diseases, she was told "It's your bad karma, the cumulative results of your past reincarnations. The evil of your past lives is taking its toll." For two years Usha had stoically endured this isolation and discipline, but it wasn't giving the peace of mind she sought. Where should she turn next? It was at this point that she met Jesus through the guidance of the Swiss missionary.

When I heard the story, my heart was gripped. By night-fall, the burden was heavy. To me this faceless person was like a baby in a lion's den. As a brand new infant in Christ, she was surrounded by spiritual counter currents. I wrestled and groaned in prayer, literally all night for the protection and needs of this vulnerable new spiritual babe. A heavy mantle of intercession had fallen upon me for her. Not only that, I knew that somehow I had to be a participant in answering that prayer. I had to go and find her and bring her out of the temple. Never mind what my assignment was for this third term—right now I had a mission from God.

Within a couple of days of returning to Khonkaen I took a five hour ride on a provincial bus to Ubon and went right to the local church. I shared the little information I had with the Thai pastor and deaconess. Then I requested they accompany me to find the temple and find Usha. I wanted to bring her home with me to disciple her.

We took two city buses to reach the edge of town and then walked another mile or two into the forest. We finally found her one room dwelling and I called softly in the forest stillness, "Usha, Usha, are you home?" A pale frail figure, head and eyebrows

100

shaven and attired in a white robe appeared in the doorway. I was momentarily taken aback and unsure how to proceed. *This was my sister in Christ? She didn't look like it!* Within a few minutes, however, I sensed the oneness we shared in Jesus amidst a wide assortment of mental baggage from her former religions. It was the middle of Buddhist Lent and she had taken a vow to practice the disciplines and to remain there for the full three months. Her new-found faith, though contradictory to her circumstances, was not yet strong enough to break her vows. My job was clear—I would have to disciple her there at the temple grounds.

So I began trips to the temple, usually two or three days at a time, staying at the church in the city. Then I'd return to my home in Khonkaen for other ministries. In the meantime, prayer partners around the world had been alerted to intercede on Usha's behalf. I needed divine wisdom to help her untangle the motley web of teachings that bound her.

On my second visit she told me of an American Buddhist nun who had been there five years. "She's reading the Bible," she added.

"Reading the Bible? Invite her to join us. I'll come again tomorrow," I promised.

"Well, she's on a vow of silence for Lent. She won't be able to speak to anyone," Usha explained.

"Never mind, I won't make her speak. She can just listen," I suggested. The next day when I arrived, there was Kirsten waiting for me. When she started to speak I said, "It's all right. You don't have to speak if you are on a vow of silence."

"It's okay," she said. "I was tired of speaking of Buddhism. But I'm happy to speak of Jesus." Within ten minutes she was weeping and committing her heart to Christ. I had done nothing. I was simply the spiritual midwife who facilitated what God was doing.

"What about my husband?" she asked. Her English husband, Paul, had been a Buddhist monk in another province for five years. He wore the saffron robe and lived in self-denial in caves, corresponding by letters to his wife. In a recent letter he had admitted that Buddhism had given him discipline and clarity of mind, but it lacked the power of change that he was looking for.

101

"We'll have to ask the Holy Spirit to convict him," I replied. We bowed together, the two shaven heads and I, and asked for another miracle—Paul's salvation. I continued to make the long trips to the forest monastery to teach Usha and Kirsten. But I never went alone. I always had a couple of Thai deaconesses along to be praying on site as I taught. There was also the prayer backing of my missionary colleagues and hundreds of intercessors in America.

One day as I was teaching the girls I felt I was losing ground spiritually with these new disciples. Usha said, "How can I be sure God is real? I don't know if I really believe in all this." Enemy darts of doubt were finding their way into her heart. The unbelief was contagious and the other nun began expressing doubts as well. I stopped immediately and in the name of Jesus verbally bound a spirit of unbelief, then witchcraft, occultism, Hinduism and others. Usha cried. The next day she told me "I feel like the plug was pulled out in a bathtub. Something went out." I then discovered that my two Thai friends who had sat on a nearby log to pray had dozed off, and the enemy had taken advantage.

As long as the three westerners were in their Buddhist robes, the temple provided them with religious study visas. Kirsten wanted to leave the temple, but felt she had to wait until her husband would do so. Otherwise her visa would expire and she would have to leave the country without him. God omnipotently met Paul and he too decided to follow Christ. A prayer alert was sent out that permission would be given and that the abbot would even help them leave. And that's exactly what God did! When the couple went to request permission the head abbot said, "You found what you came here looking for, the truth. You can leave with my blessing." They were free at last.

Paul and Kirsten went to India where they had friends. They needed time to reconnect with each other as well as to let their hair grow out again. They had been married in Thailand some six years before in a Buddhist ceremony. Now in India they chose to be remarried as Christians. Exactly one year from the day of their release from the temple their daughter was born--December 4, 1981. Returning to live in America they grew in their faith. Eventually in 1993 they returned to India—this time as dorm parents for Woodstock Christian School in the Himalayas.

For Usha although Buddhist Lent was over, she was not yet ready to leave the cloistered life of the temple. I told her whenever she wanted to leave to telegram me and I'd come and get her. Just before Thanksgiving Day the telegram arrived, "Ready to leave, Usha."

I hurried off to Ubon immediately to find her. It was November 23, 1980. She was joyous but shaken. During her final days in the forest monastery she had battled evil spirit forces. The demonic attacks were particularly violent when she burned pictures and items from her former Hindu masters under whom she had studied and worshipped. At one point, half of her face was swollen by the demonic attack. "They tried to get my soul, but could only hurt my body," she explained.

Bringing her back to stay with me, I found myself in nearly 24 hour discipleship. Daily we studied the Gospel of Mark together for three or four hours at a time. In ten days we finished the entire book. Usha eventually returned to Germany and saw her sister accept Christ. She joined the Monastery of St. John the Baptist in Essex, England. On my third furlough, I stopped in Europe to visit her—now renamed Sister Joanna. Her days and energies are spent in thoughtful work and prayer, but this time Jesus is the center.

I thought that after these three had come to Christ my job at the temple was finished. But the Holy Spirit nudged me to go again. I never went presumptuously, but always had heavy prayer backing. I took a Thai deaconess with me when I visited the Thai nuns. I had met the head nun, to whom Kirsten had given a Thai New Testament when she left the temple. Within six weeks she had read it cover to cover. I told her I wanted to give literature to all 60 of her nuns for New Years, the traditional gift giving time in Thailand. She gave permission and even helped me to distribute the Gospels and tracts herself. One Thai nun grew very fond of me and began addressing me by the pronouns and vocabulary reserved for their own nuns. She said, "You have an ordained heart like we have. You just haven't shaved your head."

The first western monk I had met when I began visiting the temples was from Brooklyn, New York. "How long have you been a monk?" I inquired as we met on a shaded forest path.

"Nine years," was his simple reply. I reflected on my own last nine years. They were full of adventure and fulfillment. He had had a routine of one meal a day from his alms bowl, sitting in meditation and walking in meditation—*nine years* of that!

"Did you ever have any church affiliation?" I continued carefully.

"My parents were Jewish," he hesitatingly responded.

I was taken aback. "Have you ever read the Bible? The New Testament? Did you know that Jesus is your Messiah?"

"No one ever told me that," he answered sadly. Tears began running down my cheeks. Knowing that what he was really seeking was Jesus, I asked him to please read the Bible again. Then standing there on the forested path in the monastery, I prayed aloud for him to some day find Jesus.

One monk that I visited perhaps more often than others was a Canadian, the abbot of a branch temple. The Lord always provided an American Christian male companion to accompany me on these visits as it would not really be proper for me as a woman to go alone. Sometimes it was a member of the Peace Corps, a refugee relief worker or a missionary's high school age son. I would say to the abbot, "Pasano, this is Mike. He is with the Peace Corps in Khonkaen." Then I would start asking the abbot questions keeping attention away from me. I avoided revealing my missionary status as long as possible in order to keep the opportunity open for communication.

After my first visit with Abbot Pasano I said, "I'd like to pray for you." He didn't say anything and I really didn't give him any chance to object. I simply prayed God's blessing upon him to find the Truth. The next visit when I suggested I would pray he said, "Please." On a third visit he said, "Thank you" after I had prayed at the close of my conversation. It was a bit incongruous to me as supposedly the monks are not to thank a person. It cancels out whatever merit the person would derive from what was done or given!

I knew that eventually someone would guess my identity. One day I was visiting Christine, a newly ordained Buddhist nun from Switzerland at the branch temple. We were standing in the semi-shade of a large-leafed forest tree. Her fair complexion was dotted with innumerable red splotches where opportunistic mosquitoes had bitten her. Little beads of perspiration glistened on her shaved head and forehead as she talked. In a momentary lull of conversation she asked me, "And what do you do in Thailand?"

I matter-of-factly stated, "Oh, I am a Christian missionary here," and continued our conversation leaving her no room to withdraw from our verbal exchange. She was obviously quite taken aback to find that a missionary would visit a Buddhist temple. Buddhism as a philosophy was never something I had an interest in. I was far from my comfort zone in visiting the temple, but it was a ministry the Lord had definitely lead me into.

For the next couple of years as I made these visits, God brought a variety of people across my path. Kay, an American traveler and visitor to that temple came through Khonkaen and needed a place to stay for the night. I invited her in and she poured out her story. She had spent several days observing temple life. She had obediently stayed 300 paces behind the silent pensive monks who had single-filed through the nearby village on their daily six a.m. alms rounds. The villagers reverently dished out scoops of steamed rice and ladles of hot curry and stir-fried vegetables into the alms bowls.

Back at the temple as a guest, she was allowed to eat the monks' leftovers, usually a blob of glutinous rice, a spoonful of re-boiled rice or a chunk of coconut rice. At night her sleep was disturbed by nightmares of the "pickled baby" as she referred to the nine-month stillborn infant preserved in a glass jar at the altar of Buddhist images in the temple. This specimen, as well as a skeleton of a 38 year old local woman, was displayed to remind worshippers of the impermanence of their bodies.

One afternoon in Khonkaen I had a surprise guest at my doorstep. It was Christine, the Swiss Buddhist nun I had met at the temple on my last visit. She still had the New Testament I had given her. Probably every western monk and nun had a pocket sized New Testament by this time because we had given them out freely. Christine was on her way to visit another Buddhist temple in the north and just needed a night's lodging. Outwardly, there were no further results from the months of visiting the temple.

However for nearly a year, I found myself praying for the Supreme Patriarch of Thailand. He was the ecclesiastical head for all Buddhism in the country. My burden was that someone would give him a Bible. I knew that on several occasions through the years Bibles had been presented to members of the Royal Family. Yet, to everyone's knowledge the religious leader had never been a recipient of a Bible.

I knew only that the Patriarch resided in some temple in Bangkok. I also knew that a woman could not directly hand anything to him nor any other Buddhist monk. There would always have to be a layman go between. The only other option was for a woman to lay an offered object on a cloth and the monk could retrieve the item from the "neutral" place.

On a public bus or train monks were given either a front seat or the back seat to help them preserve their religious purity. Either place would enable women to get on or off the bus without unintentionally brushing against their saffron robes. Although I usually preferred a front seat, I rarely chose it. I wanted to avoid the indignity of being asked to give up my seat for a monk who might be boarding at a later stop.

It was November, 1982 and I had to go to the railway station in Khonkaen to buy advance tickets for visiting mission board leaders. When I arrived I was surprised to find the usually drab rust-brown and cream colored depot festooned with bright yellow banners and ribbons. "Who is special? What is this all about?" I queried as I purchased the tickets.

"The Supreme Patriarch is here from Bangkok. Tonight he is returning on the express train." My heart skipped a beat! Was this God's doing? Was He giving me the opportunity to give a Bible to him?

I looked at my watch. It was 4:30 p.m. The one Christian bookstore in town would be closed. I hurried over anyway, praying it would still be open. Praise the Lord! The manager was witnessing to a young man and had not yet locked up. I breathlessly ran in, "I need the nicest Bible you have. The Supreme Patriarch is in town and I want to give it to him tonight." I was met with a puzzled expression and then a caution.

"Don't wrap it up. They might think it is a bomb or explosive and not receive it." I thanked her and ran home with the Bible.

Immediately I phoned a couple of local prayer partners, "Pray! I don't know how to do it, but I sense this is God's timing." On the cover leaf of the Bible I carefully penned in Thai John 8:32 "You will know the truth." Then I placed a marker at the page and underlined verse 32. I tied a simple yellow ribbon around God's Powerful Explosive. My partners and I were praying intensely and hardly daring to believe that our chance had really come.

Going down to the depot that evening I found crowds of well-wishers and worshippers awaiting the appearance of the elderly Supreme Patriarch. Then he emerged to stand on the outer platform of the train. With a bristle broom (bundle of reeds) in his hand, he was sprinkling holy water on groups of devotees as they bowed before him.

Now what do I do? I wondered. *I don't want any ceremonial water on me.* I certainly didn't want to bow either. Then I saw my chance. His assistant was a layman in street clothes standing beside him. As one group of devotees rose up to move out and make room for the next group of devotees, I darted in at the side. I politely handed the Bible to the layman and said, "Please give this to the revered Supreme Patriarch." Once again God had opened the way to be a participant to what was on His heart. [Some years later the Bible Society distributed Bibles to all the temples in Thailand.]

15—Commuter Missionary

Intercession for ministries in the temple was only a small part, almost a sideline, of what God had for me during my third term of service. My official assignment was "field-wide ministries" a nebulous catch-all. It did give me the freedom I needed to follow the Lord's leading. I later came to call those my commuter missionary days as I traveled to all provinces of northeast Thailand.

Sometimes daily, sometimes just three mornings a week, two or three ladies would partner with me for prayer at 5:30 a.m. We represented totally different ministries, but God bonded us together to pray for each other's work and over all concerns. Our hearts were so knit that even today when we meet we can instantly pray for any subject. Mrs. K was ethnic Laotian, Mrs. V was ethnic Chinese and Miss J was Thai. Having these close national peers I never really missed having a missionary coworker.

Occasionally through the years, various missionaries had attempted to begin a women's ministry that would encompass all of the northeast provinces where the C&MA was working. Somehow it had not been the Lord's timing. For months our morning prayer sessions heavily centered on the need for a women's retreat. Then one of our partners, Mrs. K who was the Christian book store manager, and three of her friends (a bakery owner, a teacher, and a local pastor's wife) took up the challenge to organize an all northeast women's conference.

There was not a single cent on hand—just faith that God was about to do something *big*. In four months of fervent prayer and advertising God brought in $1,360.

The first gift was $10 from a most unexpected source—leprous Christians. Alliance Women's groups in Ohio also heard about the plans and donated $400.

September 22, 1982 was the historic day that 200 ladies found their way to the Bible School campus for the first northeast Thailand women's retreat. All but one of the 17 provinces was represented. The registration fee of $1.25 was set low enough to enable all ladies to come. In spite of heavy rains and floods, they came by bus and train and hired truck. It was no small miracle that for once their husbands had been persuaded to care for the children so their wives could go. The opening night was celebrated with a gigantic cake two feet by five and a half feet and decorated in pink and white frosting. A special prize was awarded the first arrivals—two ladies who, in their excitement, had mistakenly arrived August 22, a whole month early for retreat. (They even had their pillows and grass sleeping mats in tow!) Two dedicated male professional cooks rose at 3:00 a.m. every day to start steaming rice for the 7:30 a.m. breakfast and to prepare a tantalizing menu throughout the retreat.

For four days the morning exercise hour and afternoon game time released gales of laughter and pent-up emotions of ladies 20 to 90 years of age. Sophistication was set aside for the "fat ladies' running walk" and the "duck waddle." A 60 year old woman, a Christian of only a month, testified, "Before I became a Christian my life was only sorrow and sadness. My husband and children died. But now Christ has given me joy and laughter." The ladies drank in the teaching and preaching sessions. Heavy prayer support on site as well as by prayer partners in America, enabled the four organizers to pull off a fantastic women's meeting. It was just the beginning of over ten years' of interdenominational ministry. The attendance grew to 500, and at one point even topped 700.

Early July in 1981 I had a phone call, "Joy, your friend had a motorbike accident and is in the hospital." It was our Dutch single lady missionary doctor who had left her home at the Khonkaen University that morning to drive her motorbike down the highway to town. She was not wearing her helmet and how the accident happened no one will ever know. There were no witnesses. She was found at the side of the road with head injuries, her ear evidently severed by some sharp object supposedly sticking out of a passing vehicle. Providentially it was one of her medical student friends who found her and rushed her to the university hospital for immediate surgery. It was late afternoon before someone at the hospital managed to notify any of us missionaries of the accident.

For nearly six weeks three of us mission nurses plus a Thai nurse gave attention to our colleague's personal needs both in the Khonkaen University hospital and later in Bangkok when brain surgery was required. Finally she was able to be medically evacuated to Holland for further care. Although the doctor predicted she would only live a vegetable-like life, God enabled her to function almost normally and live on a permanent Dutch disability allowance.

It was a lesson which re-emphasized to us fellow missionaries that when riding a motorbike one should always wear a helmet. For me as a single woman I saw the need of a designated caretaker in case of incapacity. Being on the other side of the world from my family I have since then always kept a statement on file in the mission office. "In the immediate absence of family _____ is authorized to make decisions concerning my condition." I had taken the risks and made the decisions for my doctor friend without her prior written authorization until her sister could come.

About this time a missionary couple in the next province to me was retiring. A married couple in another province and two of us single girls were assigned to commute to Chaiyapoom on alternate weekends to work with the Thai city pastor. This Chaiyapoom city church building was one of the North American Women's Missionary Prayer Fellowship portable chapel projects. My job was to train the children's Sunday School teachers.

The pastor's youngest son, Levi, was only three years old and he had a special attachment to me. He wanted to be wherever I was. He followed me into the church building one morning where I sat to quietly pray and meditate. After some minutes he began to play and run around the sanctuary. "Levi, Levi, we don't run in God's house," I firmly reprimanded. His brown eyes grew big and he immediately came and sat beside me.

After some minutes of silence he whispered softly, "But where is God? I don't see Him!"

I never guessed the extent of his hero worship until his mother told me one day. "Levi, wouldn't let me cut his hair this week. He said he wanted long hair like Ma'am Joy. He put a towel over his head like the scarf you wear." It was an illustration I would often use in training Sunday School teachers through the years. "A teacher is not just a teacher one hour on Sunday morning. Little eyes and ears learn from you 24 hours a day."

Every summer Thailand missionaries welcomed Alliance Youth Corps (AYC) girls and fellows for seven weeks of hands-on missionary experience. I was sometimes the coordinator of their schedules. On occasion I had included Chaiyapoom for their ministry. The bus route there ran on a two hourly schedule and the bus always full to overflowing. One day I had to take that bus when I was escorting two AYC boys. We arrived at the bus station half an hour early to make sure we would get good seats. But I was startled to find the bus already crammed with passengers. They were mostly students going for a pre-entrance exam. We had no choice but to take a deep breath, squeeze in and stand in what little space was left of the bus aisle.

The bus pulled out ten minutes early (a historical first, I'm sure!) and outside of town stopped for about three minutes. I suddenly realized that I could breathe a bit easier. Twenty or more passengers—all boys—had climbed out and onto the roof of the bus. To my consternation one was an AYC boy. He was glad for the good view and air where he could read his book—until it started to rain.

As we approached a town, the roof passengers were in-structed to get inside again so the driver would not get a ticket. At another point the driver turned off his blaring radio and forbade anyone to breathe a word. We were passing a highway police booth. He wanted to pass unnoticed for fear he would be cited as overloaded. He landed only one ticket in the two hour drive.

My parents had left Thailand in 1974 after 28 years of ministry, in order to care for my elderly grandparents. An only child, Dad had no siblings to share the responsibility. They anticipated only a couple years hiatus, but were never able to return to their missionary work since my grandparents lived to 89 and 97. We five children knew how deeply Mother and Dad missed Thailand. After Grandpa Boese died in May, 1982, we conferred by mail. We announced that in honor of their upcoming 40th wedding anniversary, Mother and Dad could have an all expense paid trip to Thailand. Their kids and grandkids were saving for it.

Dad had been field chairman for many years when we were young and as a family we had traveled extensively throughout the provinces. Now having been away for eight years my parents were excited to visit the Christians again and see what progress had been made. Their first thrill was to meet Beth Limare, our first Filipina missionary, who had recently arrived for language study. Their next joy was to meet my prayer partner, Vaneda, who had started Chinese Alliance churches in the northeast. She paved the way for Chinese in Hong Kong to send more missionaries to Thailand.

For 63 days my parents and I traveled by every conceivable means of public transportation—pony cart and roofless three wheeled pedicab included. We visited 57 churches. At one church we observed a Christmas program that was a two hour dramatized sermon depicting the life of Christ. We chuckled as Lazarus shook to death from a malaria attack and was buried in the empty church baptistery. He came to life again with a wool blanket over his head. At this Mary's and Martha's friends were so frightened they ran off the stage screaming, "A ghost, a ghost!"

I took my parents to visit the Thai Buddhist nuns in the forest monastery in Ubon where I had ministered frequently. The nuns were amazed to discover that my mother (respected for her age and graying hair) believed in Jesus too. It was quite an arresting thought to them. It was just as incongruous to us that the western Buddhist monks and nuns were celebrating Christmas! There were about ten of them from Australia, Canada and America.

Although my whole third term of ministry was busy working with village women's meetings, holding seminars for Sunday School teacher training, coordinating AYC, commuting to city churches for ministry and making temple visits, I knew my real ministry had been learning to be an intercessor. It seemed to be what I came to call crisis intercession. Urgent needs were often a call to intense and concentrated prayer until an answer was forthcoming.

I was finishing the last year of this my third term when yet another issue reared its head. For some years we had had short term mission teams of ten to twenty young people from many denominations come from Singapore and Hong Kong to visit us in Khonkaen. We missionaries served as hosts, interpreters, advisors, tour guides and resource persons. In one group was a young Singaporean policeman who had been assigned as Billy Graham's personal security guard during an evangelistic crusade in his country in 1978.

His fiancée was a government worker and member of another church and had come along. They asked me an unexpected question, "Joy, why aren't you married?"

I gave my usual answer, "I love being single. I don't have the time or the desire to be married. Maybe when I retire if I'm lonesome I'll marry to have someone to talk to. Whenever there's a snake around or a flat tire there is always someone's husband to take care of it. I don't need a husband!"

"You need to pray about it. We are going to pray for a husband for you."

"Go ahead. It won't make any difference," I laughed. The day after they left I was reading in Genesis in my personal devotions. It was the familiar story of Abraham offering up his beloved Isaac on the altar. Suddenly I was deeply convicted. Singleness had become my idol. I was shocked and embarrassed before God. I struggled, not wanting to put my singleness on the altar. I feared I would have to get married and give up my freedom and happiness. I cried. Finally I surrendered, "Lord, forgive me for having this idol. I'm willing to be married if that's Your will, but You'll have to make me happy about it."

I was at peace and thought to myself, *I'm safe. There are no marriageable men on this mission field. "He" would have to be 40ish and a missionary.* In the Lord's sense of humor He proceeded to test my commitment. Ironically, no less than six eligible bachelors came across my path in the next few months. They were of other missions or refugee organizations. I was surprised and held my breath. But to my relief there was no interest.

It was with a little anxiety that I prepared to go home for furlough. I knew that America had many unattached men. My whole life could change. I decided I would need to do all the traveling I wanted, because if I got married, a husband might slow me down!

So it was that at the end of my missionary speaking tour in Hawaii (my second time) that I took the opportunity to extend my travels on down to Australia. My brother had just moved to

Sydney to be an assistant pastor in a Baptist church so I wanted to visit him and see a little of Australia. I also had several days in New Zealand to see American pastor friends and meet a group of Alliance Women in Auckland. They had been particularly supportive in prayer, letters and occasional parcels during my second term in Khonkaen. This was the first of my four visits "Down Under."

As long as I could remember I had planned my life months and years in advance. But unexplainably I found a blank after the end of 1984. It was as though God would not allow me to make any more plans. Was I getting married? What was around the corner?

Over the new year I seemed to hear *two years* as a small voice in my heart. *Two years? Two years, what*? I puzzled. But it persisted. Finally one morning in my devotions I said, "Lord, if You are only releasing me to return to Thailand for two years please put it in writing. As I read my Bible this morning please have the word *two* twice in the chapters I read to confirm this is You speaking." I ordinarily read three or four chapters and was somewhere in Chronicles. Moments later my heart melted under the unmistakable answer from God. In the very first chapter I read *two years* not twice but four times! God wanted to make sure I got the answer.

I was in a quandary over what the mission board would say. Carefully explaining the whole episode to my mission leaders later that month, I summed it up, "God has only given me permission to return to Thailand for two years. I don't know why. He has not said." Their answer was partially tongue in cheek.

"At the end of two years read those verses again, Joy. Then you can stay a second two years. Otherwise you know the rule. You'll have to pay back half your outfit and your travel home." And so it was on those terms that I returned to Thailand for my fourth term.

As my two years back on the field came to a close I wondered what the Lord had to say to me. It was 1987 and the C&MA was celebrating the centennial of our denomination. The missionaries were encouraged to plan vacations in the homeland to join in the celebration. Then I realized that I would never have even considered going home for any reason before my four year

114

term was up. I was on the mission field to work. Spending money on me had never come easily. A trip home for vacation seemed like an extravagance to me. Yet it had been so clear and direct from the Lord that I was to return in two years.

I bought my ticket and flew home to enjoy my family and a wonderful historic centennial council in St. Paul, Minnesota. It was as if the Lord wanted me to enjoy His abundance. He had provided abundant life and I was only focused on spiritual things. I needed that balance.

For three terms I had lived in Khonkaen province. Now my fourth term assignment was Sisaket, a city of 31,000 people on the Cambodia-Thailand border. This city was not unlike the other Thai towns I had lived in but it was on a smaller scale. When I had to move my personal belongings and mission furniture from the storage rooms in Khonkaen to Sisaket a missionary man kindly accompanied me. We sat in the cab with the driver of the ten wheel freight truck for seven hours. It was quite an unpleasant hot, sticky and dusty ride. That night the missionary man stayed in the town's best hotel. About midnight he got up for a drink of water and found the bathroom floor flooded with five inches of water. In fact, the bedroom and hallway were also flooding. A water pipe to the toilet had broken. The hotel help were called and they used his towels to mop up the floor. The water was then turned off for the entire floor for the rest of the night. The missionary never did get his drink of water and in the morning had no water for a shower or to shave. Needless to say he wasn't too impressed with the finest hotel in Sisaket!

After the role of commuter missionary in the villages for four years I was quite ready to settle down and focus on one church of 25 members in the city. My job was labeled "church nurture." My missionary coworker was Beth Limare, a Filipina in the last year of her first term. Beth and I were the only missionaries in town so the pastor divided up the responsibilities. It fell to me to train the children's Sunday School teachers and play the electric organ for services. All of us would share in evangelism, visitation and discipleship.

Keeping in mind the mission principle that we were working ourselves out of a job I insisted that I would only play the organ if someone in the church would learn to play. Someday I would move on and a church member would need to take over the music. Four people readily agreed to learn. I had never taught anyone to play the organ or read music notes before. I didn't know what to call the notes in Thai and made up my own words. A young girl gave up quickly when she found that lessons alone were not enough. She had never considered that she might need to practice between lessons! A teenager wanted to play chords without learning the notes. The other two students were married women who needed short cuts and early successes to motivate them. After a year they both managed to play simple hymns for an offertory in church.

Beth rode a motorbike and despite my acute dislike for them I rode sidesaddle behind her. Only once did we have a little tumble. A child on a bicycle cut in front of us suddenly and sent us sprawling on the rough asphalt. The child was fine, but we both had our knees skinned. I carry scars to this day from that misadventure. I preferred the lumbering local bus, a three wheeled pedicab or my bicycle for transportation. The small sleepy town of friendly people where the church, market, post office, hospital, train station and bank was all within walking distance—that was Sisaket. It was a refreshing change from the hustle and bustle of Khonkaen with its population of 214,000.

Within a relatively short few months several new people came to Christ and a baptismal service was held at the city reservoir. At their request the two invalid women were each carried by four men down into the water for full immersion.

A Thai couple in their late 40's or early 50's who lived twenty minutes down the train line from town had listened to the Gospel on radio. They wrote to the Christian station to find out where the nearest church was, and were referred to us. Because the husband was a nurse who ran a private clinic in the mornings, they couldn't come to Sunday morning worship. Instead they came to Wednesday evening prayer meetings, returning home on the night express train. It wasn't very many weeks before they both accepted Christ. The wife then shared the Gospel with her widowed sister, Mrs. SJ, who had eight children.

So one Sunday morning Mrs. SJ, with her three youngest children, appeared shyly under the shady sea almond tree at church. Although their clothes were old and worn, everyone was spotlessly clean. For the next few weeks they sat attentively in my inquirers' Sunday School class while I shared the plan of salvation. As usual I began with the story of creation, followed by Noah, the Old Testament prophecies and finally the life of Christ. On the Sunday of baptism a couple months later Mrs. SJ brought her extra skirt and towel in preparation for baptism. "But you have

117

not prayed to receive Jesus yet. You can't be baptized until you are a Christian," I explained.

"Well, I believed my second Sunday. I had painful and stiff knees. Jesus healed them so I believed," she countered. I felt chided and suggested we officially pray the sinners prayer there in the Sunday School class and then see what the pastor had to say. He understood his people and was happy to baptize her along with her sister's family who had believed earlier.

I began discipling Mrs. SJ in her home. It was a simple one room concrete block structure with a dirt floor, slum housing at the edge of town, to be more exact! Every Wednesday afternoon, rain or shine I'd go and teach her from the Gospel of John. Later it was the Book of Acts that we studied. She was an eager learner and zealous to witness. Soon neighbors joined us and a Gospel chain developed as one by one they accepted Christ.

One of her neighbors was Auntie Pong, who had lived a life of promiscuity and now was dying of uterine cancer and venereal disease. In the local hospital she was placed in the room furthest down the hall yet the putrid odor of her rotting flesh wafted all the way to the nurses' desk. Finally she was sent home to die. Her teenage son, Ak loyally cared for his poverty stricken mother and slept under a filthy mosquito net on the hard earth floor with her at night. My colleague and I could hardly keep from gagging on the odor as we visited her regularly, reading scripture and praying with this new Christian.

We knew Auntie Pong's end was near but we had to leave town for some important meetings. As soon as we returned, we hurried to Auntie Pong's hovel, only to find it empty. She had died the day before. A neighbor woman told us to which temple her body had been taken. We went directly to see how the young son was doing. The few relatives gathered there were so relieved to see us. "We didn't know what Christians do for funeral ceremonies. We hope it is okay. We washed the body ceremonially and have had the monks chant. Can you do a Christian ceremony here in the temple pavilion now?"

We couldn't pass up the opportunity. We hurried to the church. But the pastor was out of town so we gathered some hymnals and Bibles and stopped to tell the elder and those church members we could find. Back at the temple pavilion we assembled ourselves on grass mats around on the floor in front of the simple unadorned coffin. A monk seated nearby on an elevated platform turned out to be her estranged husband. An elder read the scripture and I explained that for a Christian Jesus takes His child home at the last breath. It was great comfort for Ak, a new Christian, as well as all the non-Christian relatives. We stayed and witnessed and gave out Gospel tracts to everyone. The next day we returned to be a moral support and comfort to Ak during the cremation ceremony.

Mrs. SJ's son, Pongsuk, was only nine years old but he was a good pal to Ak. Both boys attended church regularly but Pongsuk still had not accepted Christ. He had listened attentively to all the teaching in the inquirers' class. And even though his mother and two younger sisters prayed to receive Christ he said he wasn't ready yet. He didn't know if God was really real. As a widow Mrs. SJ found it hard to feed her brood of eight fatherless children and sometimes had to send the young ones off to school hungry. Pongsuk himself had to walk five miles to his school.

One day when Pongsuk had eaten no breakfast and it was nearing noon time, his stomach was rumbling with hunger pains. He decided to try prayer, "God, if You are real could You please help me? I'm so hungry and I have nothing to eat. Could You please help me find food or else make me not hungry?"

Just then a school buddy called, "Pongsuk, have you eaten?" He shook his head shyly. "Come then. I'll treat you to a bowl of noodles." Now he knew God was real and had heard his prayers.

Walking home from school that day Pongsuk stopped by my house and rang the doorbell. "I want to invite Jesus into my heart. Now I know God is real," he explained. A simple bowl of noodles had convinced him.

Almost every day Beth and I would walk to church for an early morning prayer meeting with the pastor and staff. One of our prayers was that we could have more contact with the middle class professionals. God answered in an amusing way. It was time to renew Beth's motorbike license and I went along with her to the government office. Looking for conversation I casually said, "I only have a bicycle. Guess I don't need a license for that."

"Oh yes, you do. Here, see mine?" The middle-aged police officer countered. I was quite surprised as I looked at the tattered yellow piece of paper the official held out to me. "You go over to that other building over there and fill in the papers. It only costs four cents."

"Do you mean to tell me that all these school kids riding bikes have a license?" I asked incredulously.

"Those that have licenses do and those that don't, don't," was the incongruous reply. Beth and I chuckled to ourselves.

"Let's go. It's another chance to interact with government officials," we told ourselves.

A policeman ushered us upstairs to the proper office where a somewhat inebriated officer wearing dark glasses fumbled through files looking for the form. Somehow I didn't write something correctly on the first form and he crumpled it up giving me a fresh one. I still didn't do it to his satisfaction on the second try. On the third try he took over and proceeded to fill it in on my behalf. After I had signed and paid my four cent fee he took it downstairs to his superior to sign.

Soon he was back explaining, "The boss is in a meeting so just relax here a while." After an hour of small talk he went downstairs again and returned with complimentary soft drinks for Beth and me. We both knew it cost twenty cents a bottle. It was another hour before the required signature was forthcoming. In lieu of my photo, a thumb print was required. The printed caution on the tiny license said, "Memorize your number in case of loss." My number was three! "Just a minute," the officer said, as we got up to leave. "I have to give you a receipt. The boss has to sign that as well."

It was all we could do to keep from rolling with laughter. We had spent two hours and four cents to get my life time bicycle driver's license. The police department had spent three forms and forty cents for soft drinks for us to fulfill an ancient law that had never been taken off the books and was seldom enforced. But the whole episode was an answer to our prayer. We had taken opportunity to witness and hand out tracts to government officials.

For years I had my dentistry done in a mission hospital in central Thailand. Then one day in Khonkaen I had an urgent dental problem and could not take time to make the two or three day trip to reach my dentist. I heard of other colleagues who were satisfied with a local dentist. I went to find the clinic and was surprised to find the dentist kept a huge German shepherd dog in his office. I really didn't mind. Dogs I loved but dentists I avoided.

With my ordeal over, I noticed a Christian magazine in his waiting room. The dentist explained that his daughter in America had sent it to him. Very pleased to hear this, I hurried to find my prayer partner, Vaneda. "There's a Chinese dentist here you need to visit and witness to," I said. The end result was that eventually he and his wife accepted Christ and joined the Chinese Church in Khonkaen.

In the meantime two missionary coworkers happened to ask me about a good dentist—did I know any? I sang the praises of this man and how gentle he was. "Are you sure he's a real dentist and not a quack like so many?" asked one potential patient.

"Well, I didn't ask where he trained and I didn't look for a diploma," I admitted. "You can see for yourself. Missionary C has been very happy with his work."

After two more satisfied and impressed missionary patients, the dentist wondered out loud to one of them, "Why are Americans coming to me? I'm not even trained. My father was a dentist in Laos and I just watched him. I have to be extra careful so I don't do the wrong thing." It was a surprising discovery and even more so that he was not Missionary C's dentist after all! From the start I had walked into the wrong office! But it was obviously God's choice.

A few years later in Sisaket when a filling fell out I knew I couldn't take the seven hour trip to Khonkaen to my non-dentist. I decided I would have to take my chances locally. I walked into a dentist office in town. There was no one in the waiting room and without so much as asking my name or making any record I was ushered to the dental chair. "My filling fell out," I said to the dentist-looking man who never introduced himself but began work. He was just finishing up when a thunderstorm knocked out the electricity. The windowless room was left pitch dark. The dental assistant grabbed a flashlight and beamed it into my gaping mouth.

"Get that mosquito out of there," barked the dentist. (I suppose the intruder was making a supervisory check on my filling.) I paid my four dollars and was finished. As usual this was another opportunity to give a Gospel tract. I never did find out his name or if he was really a dentist or not.

I was never without Gospel tracts when I left the house. Virtually 99% of the people I met did not know Christ so every occasion was an opportunity to sow another seed. The three wheeled pedicab drivers I patronized were frequent recipients of tracts. One day I was walking home from the post office and a pedicab driver begged me to let him pedal me home. He said he would even take me free of charge. I explained I really didn't need a ride; I wanted the exercise. "Well, then could you give me one of those papers that tell about the guy who died and came to life again?" Oh, that was it, I realized. He wanted a Gospel tract!

"Sure, if you'll stop by the house or church I'll give you a whole book free." I offered. Gospels of John and Mark were kept in good supply.

In Khonkaen I had adopted the custom of a British missionary family. They prepared literature gift packets for their friends at New Years time. In Sisaket we expanded it. As a church we put together hundreds of attractive packets. There was a Gospel of Luke, tracts, and a booklet on the meaning of Christmas. Then we distributed them to the government offices. Some years the gift was coupled with an invitation to a special church program.

Church nurturing in Sisaket was a double thrust. On one hand we reached out to the throngs of unsaved at every level. On the other hand we fed the small flock of believers. Our ministry team divided the home Bible studies among us. Beth and I would ride a rickety old pedicab whose wheels were nearly falling off, to the shrimp chip factory on Saturday nights. After Bible study in Genesis the host would drive us home in his BMW!

Tuesday nights there was a Romans study at the restaurant owned by an elder. The study started at 8:00 p.m. after the floors had been cleaned and the chairs stacked upside down on the tables. Knowing that he had boasted to his neighbors, "Christians are on time and keep their word," we were never late.

Wednesday afternoon Bible Study was in Mrs. SJ's slum area dwelling. One day she told me, "Some Christians came to visit me from Ubon. They told me I wasn't going to heaven as I wasn't one of the 144,000 chosen. I told them I didn't know who Jehovah was but I know Jesus will take me to heaven when I die because Ma'am Joy said so." Yes, Jesus was real to the Christians in Sisaket.

17—A Forever Friend

My autobiography would be incomplete if I did not mention elephants. From childhood I had been enamored with the huge gentle beasts. I seemed to have an eye for elephants and could spot them on a city street or open highway long before anyone else. They were the tamed ones always with a mahout, straddling the neck. Given a gentle nudge of the trainer's foot behind the mammoth ear, the elephant knew to turn in that direction. Elephants have little eyes but great power and strength in that trunk swaying continuously in search of edibles! I never ceased to be amazed at God's creation.

Through the years I had managed a few elephant rides. Once while taking a short cut to church on a village road I came upon an elephant giving rides to children. I parked the Land Rover and climbed out to walk beside my giant friend, patting his leg or trunk affectionately. Although I was dressed Thai style in a wrap around skirt I managed to clamber into the riding basket from the second floor porch of a villager's home. The pleased mahout gave me an extra long ride for my 20 cents. An American woman was unexpectedly good publicity for his business! The ten minutes over, I climbed back into the Rover and continued on to church. It was the Lord's sense of humor to drop that little pleasure into my lap on the way to Sunday morning worship.

Living in Sisaket put me just one hour away from the famous annual Elephant Round Up. Every November tourists came from around the world by train and bus to watch the show. Usually 100 elephants, including 20 babies, performed. From 7:30 a.m. until noon we watched elephant tug-of-war where one elephant competed against 70 Thai soldiers. Then there was elephant soccer and a mock reenactment of the Siamese-Burmese War on elephant back like the old days. On occasion we received choice seats free, courtesy of Dick Johnston, our own missionary colleague, who was the proficient English announcer. Afterwards I could hire an elephant taxi to go into town to catch the train home.

One evening in Sisaket I was alone in the house. It was 10 p.m. and I was already in bed when the gate buzzer rang. *Who could it be?* I wondered. *I've just moved in and don't really know people in this town yet.*

Miss D quickly introduced herself in perfect English and apologized for her late night visit. She had a personal problem and needed counsel. She trusted a missionary stranger to listen. As champion tennis player for the province of Sisaket she was well known in town and had no one in which she wanted to confide.

She had received a Rotary scholarship to do graduate studies in Essex Junction, Vermont. While there she had been befriended by Christians and taken to church. Back in Sisaket she had rubbed shoulders with missionaries—often playing tennis with Joe Doty in the afternoons. She taught English at the Physical Education College. But the gospel never seemed to penetrate beneath the surface of her heart.

Unburdening herself of her troubles that night she looked at me for a response. "The answer to your needs is Jesus," I began. "He is the only One who can change the situation. I'll pray for you. I want you to know, Miss D, that I'll be your friend. Even if you remain a Buddhist and never become a Christian, I'll be your friend. I will never pressure you. But you must understand that when I die or you die that is the end of our friendship. However, if you become a Christian, we will be friends forever in heaven. In fact, we would be sisters." She knew my offer of friendship was sincere.

For the next three years that relationship deepened. She wanted to study English with me. I consented only if it was a Bible study. She readily agreed, so my colleague and I began going to her house. She had a vivacious and enthusiastic personality. But when we sat together to read the Gospel of John she would suddenly get sleepy and yawn. We noticed this several times. "I don't know why I'm so sleepy. I'll go and wash my face," she said on one occasion. Noticing the idol shelf in the hallway, Beth and I quietly bound the powers of darkness, and Bible study progressed.

Finally one day I said, "Miss D, the reason you are sleepy is because Satan doesn't want you to study the Bible. We are going to pray." We prayed out loud in the name of Jesus binding the interference. God worked. Suddenly the sleepiness was gone.

Becoming a Christian would not be easy for her, a government teacher who was expected to model patronage of the state religion before her students. The daily gestures of worship to the image at the school gate were only a part. Every holiday and social function involved Buddhist rites of some kind. She told her students very openly, "We have freedom of religion in our country, so we need to study other religions as well. I as your teacher am investigating Christianity."

At Christmas time we were waiting at the church to go caroling when Miss D appeared. In America she had seen caroling and wanted to be a part. We had not invited her, thinking this was an outreach and she was not yet a Christian. Her participation might even be an obstacle. But she was there with her Jeep and it *was* helpful to have another vehicle to use.

Our first appointment was at the governor's mansion. We had properly delivered an official letter in advance stating that we as a church wanted to come and sing a blessing on his family for Christmas. We were duly admitted by the gate guard to the premises. The governor and family came out to the front steps and graciously greeted us. As we sang, read scripture and prayed a blessing on him he was scanning the faces of the singers. Recognizing his tennis pal, Miss D, he said, "Oh, are you one [Christian] too?"

She enthusiastically answered, "Not yet, but I'm studying." We presented the governor with a New Testament. He in turn gave each caroler a bottle of cold Pepsi and a white T-shirt!

At the chief judge's house we found a long table set in the driveway for the 16 of us. We were served hot herbal tea and fruit in response to our caroling.

We continued to witness regularly to Miss D and she even traveled with me to Bangkok to talk with Dr. Ravi Zacharias, the visiting evangelist from Canada. It intrigued her that he had given up his Hindu Indian practice for faith in Christ. But she said, "When I become a Christian, I'll be one 100%!" We never pushed her.

About two years after meeting Miss D she received a tantalizing job offer near a relative in Canada. She was restless and wanted to go. Inwardly I mourned. I had asked God to open up friendship evangelism opportunities in Sisaket. He had answered. Miss D was truly a friend and I would miss her. How would she find Christ in the materialistic west? However I knew God could reach her wherever she was.

After she left I wrote her letters, but months passed without any reply. Then one morning nearly a year later Miss D walked into my house. Without bothering to give the customary Thai greeting, she blurted out in English. "I have God in my heart! I have God in my heart! I'm your sister!" I was so excited and perplexed at what had happened.

She told me that just a few days earlier she had been in America boarding a bus back to Canada. The friends seeing her off at the station were Christian Rotary Club members she had met in Thailand. Sitting in an ice cream shop waiting for the bus they had asked her, "Don't you want to accept Jesus?" She had bowed her head then and there and invited Christ to be her Lord.

Back in Thailand Miss D was a witness wherever she went. With pedicab drivers, market vendors and government officials she openly shared her new found faith. Her mother and her sister also became Christians.

Some years down the road she fell in love with a Christian man. Her younger sister was too self conscious to be a bridesmaid in the wedding, so Miss D begged me to take her place. At age 48 I felt a bit reluctant to play the part, but then I did. After all, I was her sister!

Miss D was not my only friend. One day in the Sisaket market my colleagues Beth and Edna met a plump pleasant little woman who insisted they come to tea at her house.

Auntie S surprised them with European style goodies and table settings. Gradually her story spilled out. She had been a cultured woman of means in another part of Thailand when her business partner swindled her. In shame and financial straits, she had gone to live in Europe for a while.

In Switzerland she had gone to church twice, once when she arrived (to tell the god of the land she had come and ask for his protection) and again before she left (to say she was leaving). Back in Thailand she chose to live in the quiet town of Sisaket far from her own home. Sisaket had the reputation for being one of the poorest of the northeastern provinces. A newspaper had once printed a sensational report that some children had nothing to eat and ate dirt. The truth of the matter was it was a tasty clay soil which the kids snacked on. Our pastor said he had enjoyed it as a child himself.

Auntie S wanted to practice English and was lonesome for friends who had experienced life abroad. She had a sense of humor and generously offered to help in any way she could. We didn't know quite what to make of our new friend. Again the only English we offered was Bible English. That was no problem to her. She had attended Christian classes as a child and could still sing some of the songs and recite a scripture passage from Luke. She remembered that one time a Dr. Bradley, an early Presbyterian doctor in Thailand, had sewed up an injury for her.

As we began teaching the Book of John to her in her home she made detailed notes on her writing pad. She frequently came to our house to learn how I made bread and yogurt. We exchanged goodies and strengthened the bridge of friendship. At Easter time she heard we were having a sunrise service at church. Knowing it was a special occasion, she wanted to attend. To our chagrin she was the first one there and wondered where all the Christians were! The sun was up before they arrived.

One day it dawned on us that our friend Auntie S was a fortune teller. We had noticed she never wanted us to leave the Bible in her home—always urging us to take it home. We had not thought much about it. Her explanation was that it disturbed her gods. She told us she had been given special powers. She said therefore she did not charge a fee for her fortune telling. Clients would come to her with their needs and she would go into a trance to counsel them. Whatever they gave her was what she lived on.

No wonder she occasionally became glassy eyed during our Bible study, besides there would be that strange unnatural laugh. Beth and I had always gone together to her home. Now we made doubly sure we were not alone, so that one of us could pray while the other one taught. We were never invited into her "god room" as she called it. When she moved to smaller quarters her bedroom and god room were one and the same. Then we were only invited to sit on the porch.

Over and over the way of salvation was explained to her in answer to her pointed questions. The Holy Spirit gave powerful illustrations and anointed answers time and again. But it was always as if she were on the outside looking wistfully in the window. "Auntie S, your hands are so full of your good deeds there is no room for Jesus. You have to empty them and just have Jesus," I said. She shook her head sadly.

I returned to visit her and my other Sisaket friends after my fourth furlough and she gave me a royal welcome. She wanted to accompany me to all the Christians' homes as well. I asked about a promising young postal clerk we both knew. Her eyes grew troubled and she lowered her voice. "You should have been here," she said. "He was dying of a brain tumor and in such pain. He pleaded with me to help him. I prayed to the Lord Buddha to help him but it didn't do any good. I told him he needed Joy's God to help. But I didn't know how to ask Jesus."

Aware of the young man's lifestyle I asked, "Brain tumor? Are you sure it wasn't AIDS?"

"Yes, it was AIDS but no one else knows. They all think it was a brain tumor." Society was just beginning to encounter AIDS deaths and could not admit the painful diagnosis. Brain tumors and various cancers were often claimed to be the cause of death.

"I'm sorry," I said. The young man had heard the Gospel on more than one occasion but had refused it. Now it was too late.

It has been more than 15 years since that conversation and Auntie S still has not given up the filthy rags of her righteousness for the righteousness of Christ. We continue to keep in contact. Whenever she went to Bangkok she dropped in for a visit, insisting we study some more of the Book of John. A diabetic, her eyesight has degenerated. Soon it may be eternally too late and our friendship will end on this earth, while Miss D's friendship continues forever.

18—The Governor

Back in my commuter missionary days in Khonkaen I had a phone call from a Baptist missionary in Bangkok. The governor of a nearby province had just accepted Christ. Would I follow him up and disciple him? I was to go to the governor's office and introduce myself as a friend of this Baptist missionary, and I would be welcomed. False cults were already bothering this new Christian who had no knowledge of whom to trust.

I was not sure I wanted to take the assignment. As a single woman I did not think it wise to go alone to visit a man who had been separated from his wife for a number of years. Secondly, I was unsure of the proper etiquette and vocabulary to use with an official of such high position. So I found a missionary couple to accompany me.

As we entered the governor's office I was momentarily distracted by the multiple shelves of idols along one wall. *How can he be a Christian?* I wondered to myself. The governor was a man of very small stature—so short he had a box on which to rest his feet under his over-sized desk. He had a good command of English having earned his PhD in economics in the United States. His printed thesis was a hard cover book, *History of the Thai Revolution.* Even I as a native English speaker, needed a dictionary to look up some of the vocabulary in his book.

As was his custom he took us to lunch that day. Aides and body guards hovered around as he chatted easily in English. "I believe in God. I believe in Jesus Christ," he stated emphatically. It was a good first visit and I discovered that my language fears were unfounded.

My next visit was in the capacity of a member of Hospital Christian Fellowship (HCF). It had been a couple months since I had seen him. Every weekend he had been in Bangkok courting the young Christian doctor who had led him to Christ. They had a church wedding down there and now she was living in the province with him. My companion, the Thai HCF representative was also a close friend of the doctor (governor's wife) and wanted me to come along to visit. The governor was exceedingly pleased to have us come.

The governor's mansion was an old fashioned government house with high ceilings and shuttered windows. He had invited three local doctor friends over for us to witness to during supper. But the governor was so busy witnessing, we ended up listening! "You have an emptiness in your life. You need God there," he authoritatively asserted to one doctor.

The whole evening a pistol lay at the governor's right hand and an M16 rifle was in the corner. There had been unrest in the province and threats of trouble. He had a reputation for integrity and could not be bribed as so many of his predecessors had been. He lived strictly on his governor's salary and never dipped into government funds personally. After two years' administration he still had $450,000 surplus of the government budget for the province. As a result he had been highly commended as a model governor by the Prime Minister. Understandably this had not made him very popular with the other 67 provincial governors of the kingdom.

I was fascinated by all I was hearing, but ill at ease with the guns and the possibility of an attack on his life. I was also sleepy. It was 10 p.m. which was past my usual bedtime. I had not known that the governor was a night owl and just getting started. Out of the blue he asked, "Joy, do you play the organ?" He could play his electric organ even though he could not read notes. He even composed songs and a friend would write out the music. "Do you know that song about Great God?" he continued.

So it was that at 10 o'clock at night I scribbled the Thai words from memory of "How Great Thou Art" and we sang as I played the organ. Who would have dreamed of such a scene in a governor's mansion in Buddhist Thailand. It was 2 a.m. by the time my HCF friend and I tumbled into bed in the guest house next door. These were the rooms used by the Prime Minister and visiting dignitaries. It was just a bit safer than the governor's residence itself we were told.

Some months later the governor was transferred to another province. He had cleaned up corruption in one province and was needed elsewhere. He and his wife had to come to Khonkaen to catch the plane to his new post. I went to the airport to see them

131

off. As usual there were the dignitaries and body guards and soldiers for such an occasion. But the first Christian governor of Thailand welcomed us warmly. I was startled when he said to his wife, "Open your purse," and matter-of-factly dumped a handful of bullets in her purse so he could hand the flight attendant his gun unloaded. "Know what this is?" he asked, patting another well wrapped parcel. I could guess. "It's my M16," he said. I was definitely not in my comfort zone.

On a vacation the following year I made a side trip to visit the governor and his wife in his new province. Entering the home I was dismayed to find a large statue of a highly revered governor of yesteryear commanding one corner. Every visitor had lit incense sticks or candles or laid flowers in front of the statue as an act of worship. Commenting on it the governor said, "What can I do? This is government property. I cannot dispense with it. I am a government servant and must preserve its property." We did the only thing we could do. We prayed in the name of Jesus binding all powers of darkness connected with it and voiding all influence over the governor and his wife.

The governor had already experienced the power of the blood of Christ. Upon awakening one night he had sensed evil power in the bedroom and had commanded in the name of Jesus that it be gone. "The blood of Jesus protects me!" The uninvited presence vacated the room.

I was troubled because he still bowed to idols in govern-ment ceremonies. He explained, "You must understand. It is in my job description as governor. If I am remiss in my duties I could lose my job. I believe God has put me in this position to help people. I am only bowing on the outside. My heart worships God."

The Lord reminded me of II Kings 5:18-19 where Naaman had said to Elisha, "when I bow down in the temple of Rimmon, may the LORD forgive your servant for this." And Elisha said, "Go in peace." I knew I would never be in the governor's shoes. I was not the Judge. That was God's job. I was to be an encourager.

My two day visit was interspersed with Bible teaching and question answering. There had been no way to properly disciple the man. Distance and scheduling were major obstacles. A governor's day was always unpredictable. He was on call 24 hours a day seven days a week for any major emergency. One evening his wife and I accompanied him out of town to a remote spot in the countryside to check on a case of log poaching. The man was fearless, having repeatedly escaped pursuers and death plots. His wife had learned to handle a pistol, but was still nervous about this lifestyle.

One time when the governor was in Bangkok his visit co-incided with a special dinner event at which Dr. Ravi Zacharias, a well known visiting evangelist, was the featured speaker. I was delighted to have the governor and his wife as my guests for the event. He enjoyed the preaching immensely. He rarely was able to attend church anywhere because his position dictated that the honored official arrives late and nothing can start until he is there. Likewise, no one should leave before the honored one.

It was too much to expect a little church in a provincial town to follow Thai protocol. It detracted from the worship of God. So he refrained from going to church. However, if he was on business or visiting in Bangkok he could quietly duck into a back seat of the English service after it began and slip out before it was finished. The non-Thai community was not so conscious of Thai protocol and would be undisturbed. They probably would not even recognize him or know that he was there.

Back in Sisaket every few months I would phone or write a note of encouragement to the governor and his wife. One day I sensed an unusual burden of intercession for him. It was so heavy I finally called long distance to see how he was. Usually both husband and wife would come to the phone and chat easily. This particular night was different however. I sensed something was amiss. His short and guarded answers made me realize perhaps he thought his phone was bugged. I asked to speak with his wife. "Sorry, she has to sleep in another room tonight. You'll read about me in the *Bangkok Post* tomorrow." I thanked him, asked him to read Psalm 91, prayed briefly with him and hung up quickly.

Then I phoned several local prayer partners and Christian leaders asking for prayer. I didn't know what the problem was, just something life threatening. For two days the burden of intercession hung over me. It was the third day before I had details since our newspapers were always a day late. There was a report that there had been a nasty protest planned against him, but suddenly it was called off for no reason. We knew God had intervened on behalf of the governor in answer to the prayers of scores of His intercessors.

Although the governor did not have the money to travel abroad, the government sent him on a defense department fact finding trip. It was to Israel and neighboring countries. His outstanding proficiency in the English language landed him the job of interpreter for the whole delegation. He told me excitedly about his time in Israel. He was profoundly touched to view the Garden Tomb. "That's where Jesus my God was buried!" he said. "And it is empty!"

Through the years he was transferred to a number of different provinces but never did I happen to live in the same province where he was posted. In my fifth term I traveled to visit them in still another province. This would be his last post since he was approaching retirement. This province was a tough assignment, known for its powerful godfathers. One day I read in the *Bangkok Post* that he had closed four bars and houses of prostitution. Knowing he was in for heavy opposition and spiritual attack, I picked up the phone to assure him of prayer support.

"Only four bars? I closed eleven!" he said emphatically.

Later that month I made a one-day trip to visit the governor and his wife. I was shocked to find that he had been battling an unknown degenerative disease for some months. He could hardly manage to button his shirt. His gait was an unsteady shuffle. Only after he went off to work that morning did his wife pour out her heart. She felt there was an evil presence in the house. She had gathered up all the government idols in the house and stored them in the garage. There had been strange happenings in the night. Light switches flipped on or off inexplicably. A white apparition had appeared in the night at the foot of the bed. The door frame of each room had a special monk's markings. A previous governor's mother had died in the house making it haunted. "Did you ever pray through the house?" I asked.

"No, can we do it now?" she asked, her eyes troubled and pleading. The two of us went from room to room praying for the blood of Jesus Christ to cleanse it of all dark powers. There was a release of spirit and we could breathe easier. No further disturbances plagued them.

As I rode the bus back to Bangkok, I had an intense prayer burden. I closed my eyes so the passenger next to me would leave me to "sleep" and not draw me into conversation. Suddenly the prayer burden lifted and I opened my eyes to see that we had just crossed the provincial border. We were no longer in the province of the governor. It was as if there was a power boundary of counter currents.

Nine years after the governor accepted Christ, I received a call from him. It was the first time my friend had ever called me. I always called him. It was proper Thai etiquette. "Joy, I'm being baptized on Thursday. Can you come? I don't want to wait any longer." He had always said that when he was baptized he would no longer bow before idols in the official ceremonies. He was only months away from retiring from government service, but had decided he wanted to take a very public stand while still in office. He would be the first Christian governor to be baptized. I was elated. This was a long awaited day.

Immediately I phoned a couple Christian leaders I knew who would want to attend the event. I wondered how many could be present on such short notice in the middle of the week. When we arrived I was pleasantly surprised to find nearly 100 people gathered for this special occasion. Apart from his wife and her extended Christian family his only relative present was a younger brother and wife. Seeing their awkwardness I moved over to befriend them. He was vice governor of another province. "Have you ever been in a church before?" I asked carefully.

"Only for my brother's wedding. I've never seen a baptism ceremony before. Why does my brother do this? He needs to represent the majority religion. As a government official it is not right to favor a minority," he blurted out in anger.

"But Thailand is wonderful to have freedom of religion," I soothed and changed the subject to a less volatile issue.

The governor's health was deteriorating at an alarming rate. Finally he was diagnosed with a rare, incurable, degenerative motor neuron disease. My subsequent visits were heart wrenching as I saw the downward progression. Later when I went to say goodbye, I could not hold back my tears. He handed me the tissues and then prayed God's blessing on me.

God had given me a burden to pray for leaders. There were the political leaders such as the governor. There had been the religious leader—the Supreme Patriarch, and professional leaders such as Miss D, the teacher who had come to Christ. And for many years there had been another name on my list.

When my colleague had suffered her motorbike accident in 1981 she was attended to by a very fine surgeon, Dr. C, head of the neuro-surgery department of a prominent university hospital in Bangkok. After my friend's recovery the following year I accompanied her to his office. We had a chance to tell him that God, the Great Physician, had a hand in her rehabilitation.

On subsequent visits he was open to further witness. At one point he listened and asked questions for half an hour. I was particularly burdened for his salvation. Then he mentioned that before going into surgery he would pray to his neurosurgeon master teacher. When I asked where he was, he answered, "Oh, he has been dead for many years but I rely on his spirit to help me in the difficult cases in the operating room."

God burdened me to pray for these various leaders. I prayed weekly and sometimes daily for lists of unsaved as well as born again leaders. Some were men anointed of God and being used mightily. It did not matter what denomination they represented. I knew Satan's darts were poised to tumble them in an attack on the Church.

19—The Sweet and the Bitter

The last year of my term in Sisaket was difficult in several ways. The mission requested that I make a survey of the provinces in the northeast to see which places might be ripe for some new church planting. I found a Thai lady for my traveling companion and we spent several weeks traveling from city to city. I not only gathered statistics but also tried to get a spiritual pulse for Gospel receptivity. Of the twelve provinces that we surveyed there seemed to be two which were particularly noteworthy. Psychologically I was prepared to move immediately and get started on the new project.

The mission executive committee agreed with my report, and preliminary groundwork was begun to map out a strategy for the new church planting effort. However, we soon learned that the Thai couple who wanted to head the team was still a part of another organization. We had no intention of taking members away from a sister mission. By that time I had only about eight months left before my furlough. Therefore it was decided that I should remain in Sisaket to finish out my term.

Emotionally I was doing poorly. A medical checkup with a missionary doctor indicated I was on the brink of burnout. I had enjoyed the ministry too much and had not taken days off and vacations as I should have. I seemed to be a little girl always in a big hurry. Now it had caught up with me. Ordinarily I was a sociable person, but I had come to the point of not wanting to answer the phone or see anyone. I was spent.

The doctor's orders were to get away to the seaside for a six week rest. I was to totally unwind and do nothing—drop off the world if I could. I was already scheduled for a two week vacation at a Christian seaside home. Providentially they were able to accommodate me in a quiet room for the extended time. I took a big box of tissues along expecting tears to flow. To my surprise I was too uptight to cry. I had to ask the godly host couple to lay hands on me and pray that I could release the pent-up tears.

All my life I had put my emotional baggage on the back burner. I was too busy to process my emotions. Slowly the clock

137

turned back. I wept thinking of my grandmother's pain of sending me off to Siam as a toddler—her only grandchild gone for five years. I cried as my mind saw little Joy at age seven at the Bangkok airport leaving for boarding school. I could see Mother's heart was breaking. But my healing came as God showed me He was there all the time. It was as if there were more than one Jesus—one Jesus went with little Joy to Vietnam, and one Jesus stayed to comfort Mother. I could not explain it theologically. I only knew Jesus, the Great Physician, was at work in healing my bottled up emotions. By the end of six weeks the Holy Spirit had gently walked me through my 44 years, restoring my soul.

I was now glad to be all alone at my post in Sisaket to re-set my pace and change my habits. I had to break my tendency of being stingy with myself. My previous spending habit was strictly on the basis of need. If I did not really need it, I did not buy it. It had been easy to spend and give to others, but now I needed to learn to love myself. I bought a 32 cent seashell ring simply because I liked it. I realized God wanted to bring balance to my life.

I no longer jumped out of bed at 5:00 a.m. and ran all day. I made myself stay in bed until 6:00 and then thoughtfully did one thing at a time instead of juggling three things simultaneously. My landlady saw the change when I sat in the swinging chair under a tree. "Waiting for someone?" she asked.

"No, just relaxing," I answered. She had never seen me do that in three and a half years as my neighbor.

In April I received a letter from the national office of the C&MA in Colorado Springs asking me to be one of six missionaries to speak at Life '89 youth conference in Colorado. The letter said they expected about 4,000 young people to attend of which 400 might commit themselves for full time service. My first reaction was—"No! I don't connect well with youth. I am not interested." But as I prayed I knew it was another assignment from God. I was bothered by the figure—why only 400? I felt God would have me pray for 800 responses.

My missionary colleagues confirmed it. They would pray for 800 responses also. Then as I met prayer supporters in America, they too agreed. Then two ladies said they would pray for 1,000 commitments at Life '89. When the altar call was given for reapers in God's harvest fields 1,140 of the 4,800 young people stepped forward! God had abundantly answered the prayers of the many intercessors across the world.

My fall missionary tour was in Minnesota and Wisconsin. In Wausau, Wisconsin I was very conscious of a divine appointment. The pastor, his wife and I had just come home from the evening missionary meeting at church. Five minutes later a woman came running in the back porch door and sat on the couch in the living room. I paid scant attention to her, assuming it was someone they knew. Meanwhile the pastor's wife somehow thought she was *my* acquaintance. Suddenly we all realized that none of us knew who she was!

Her English language was nil. Observing her appearance, I guessed she was probably Hmong and began speaking in the northeastern Thai dialect to her. It was a language similar to her Laotian tongue. We communicated easily and her story tumbled out from trembling lips. Her husband had a knife and was chasing her. She ran out of the house barefoot and up and down the streets looking for a lighted home where she might find safety.

Of all the houses on that street God led her to the one where someone could speak her language! God's timing was perfect. I translated for the police officers. Then the pastor's wife tried to call the women's shelter in town but her story was too weird. "What do you mean a Hmong woman ran into your house and you just happened to have a missionary who could speak her language?" That night the woman found safety and shelter at the Hmong pastor's home and a chance to hear the Gospel. It was a divine appointment.

My tour partner that fall was Elsie Abrams of Peru. On the occasions when I heard her speak God began dealing with my own heart. In Peru all the missionary personnel had been pulled into Lima for a focused thrust in the capital. God was blessing and the city church was now reaching back into the villages. Then I read John Dawson's book *Taking Our Cities For God*. I knew now I was in for a change. God was calling me from rural northeast Thailand to work in the capital city of Bangkok.

When a letter came from the mission executive committee in Thailand asking if I would pray about a possible assignment in the big city I chuckled. They knew that after 20 years in rural work my heart was there. It was a surprised mission team who read my response. Before they wrote, God had already called me to Bangkok. Their request was merely a confirmation to me.

For my spring speaking tour I was sent on an inter-district assignment stretching from Seattle to Pennsylvania. I knew it would be rigorous and had been warned that there might not be any rest days. I wondered how I would weather the physical demands. Again, thanks to many faithful prayer partners, I ministered all 63 days without a day off. I paced myself, grabbing every chance to slip away to rest and re-group. It was a tough but challenging tour. My personal satisfaction was in plugging into God's health and strength and finding Him adequate to meet my needs.

Just a month before my departure for my fifth term in Thailand we had upsetting news. Dad had cancer. My mind was a whirl. *Not again, Lord!*

Back in 1972 my brother, Tim had a car accident and was hospitalized with broken bones and a wired jaw. We were all on the mission field. There I was, school nurse at Dalat and I could not even be at my brother's side when he needed me. I prayed that the nurses would be good to him and give him proper care. I had to entrust him to the Lord's care when I was so far away.

Then in February 1984 I had received word of Mother's cancer. Again I was in Khonkaen half a world away when she was in surgery. I had to entrust Mother into God's hands.

Now this—Dad's cancer was inoperable and he was 73 years old. He would have radiation, but I would have to return to the mission field before treatment even began. I could not delay my departure even one day because I was one of the few remaining missionaries with a permanent resident visa, which would be invalid if I stayed abroad more than the specified one year. I cried but I finally came to terms with it. I had found that I could trust God in many areas of my life. I would trust Him again to take care of my family's needs in my absence as well. I could trust Him for the good times as well as the tough times. He could be trusted for the sweet times of family gatherings, renewing acquaintances with supporting churches and seeing God at work in young people's lives. God was also there for the times of personal crisis and family needs.

"Lord, please help us to find our house today or at least to see it." Three of us single girls had been assigned to plant a church at the edge of Bangkok in the Nong Khaam District of about 100,000 people. There were 17 Buddhist temples in that area but only one small church of any denomination. This was our second day of house hunting and we didn't want to waste a lot of time on mundane matters. God did answer that day, giving us a spacious two story five bedroom building. It had been a restaurant and cobbler shop previously, and was located on a busy lane near a vocational school where 2,000 students passed by daily.

I was about to move into this house immediately but my missionary coworker was delayed a month. Being in a new city and a new house I was not looking forward to being alone. I knew my old prayer partner from Khonkaen days, Miss Jumpa was on a sabbatical of sorts in her home town in north Thailand. I wanted to contact her to come and be my prayer partner for a month.

In God's timing we met quite unexpectedly at a Bible college graduation in Bangkok that weekend. We talked and prayed together and she accepted my invitation. "You can stay as long as you want and I will be responsible for your food and lodging," was my open ended offer. She moved into the smallest of the five bedrooms and eventually became the acting pastor of the church God planted there long after I had moved on to another assignment. More than 15 years later she is still ministering there.

There were two immediate problems with this house however. The telephone line was on request, which we discovered meant it could be a *six year* wait. Private parties offered to sell us a phone at exorbitant prices of $1,400 to $2,000. Everyone was praying for a miracle. God did intervene and within five months we were granted a special concession as a charitable organization. For the normal $255 fee, we had our phone. Repeatedly the neighbors would say, "Being without a telephone is like being without arms and legs! Now tell me again, how did you get your telephone so fast? God really did help you."

The second problem was a very prominent spirit house in our front yard. Nearly every Thai home included a small shrine somewhere in the yard, to house the property's spirit protectors. To placate those beings, regular mini-offerings of rice, tea and bananas would be placed at the miniature temple-like house on a pedestal. As Christians, we did not want a spirit house in sight. The owner refused to remove it, even after we explained that we would not be feeding the spirits—they would probably go hungry and run away. We knew it would be offensive to cover it up, so we resorted to prayer.

Partners around the world prayed with us for a solution to the problem. I gave the Lord a number of suggestions. "Lord, could You send a vine to grow up and cover it?" But the only vines were over our back wall and had to be chopped down regularly to reduce the snake population.

"Lord, maybe You could use termites to make a mud covering over the spirit house." But the termites infested our kitchen roof instead.

"An earthquake, Lord? Just a small one to topple it naturally." Instead a motorcyclist crashed his bike into the accordion pleated metal gates of our front door.

But God gave us *His* solution. We erected a 39" x 39" tin sign to cover the gate where the spirit house stood. A professional sign painter printed in large letters: Jesus answered, "I am the way the truth and the life" (John 14:6). The angle of the gate ensured that everyone passing our house would be faced with the Word. Little school boys walking by would chant in their sing-song memorizing rhythm "Je-sus an-swered, I-am-the-way..." My bedroom was just above the gate. Even at ten o'clock at night I heard the drunks reading the sign aloud.

About every three months we would decide everyone had memorized it by now and we would change the verse. We were regular customers of the sign painter. One day when the scripture read, "Come to me, all you who are weary" (Matthew 11:28), the doorbell rang. A man was doubled over crying. "I was ready to commit suicide and I saw your sign," he sobbed. The Thai worker led him to Jesus. God had triumphed marvelously over the concrete shrine behind the sign. When we moved out of that house four years later, the sign was the last item to be removed. The neighbor man very reverently helped load it into the truck.

I wanted to sharpen my witnessing skills and found an ideal tool. Evangelism Explosion was being taught in Thai in Bangkok. It was extremely demanding on my language skills with exact word memorization. But with much prayer I passed the course and began witnessing. "Do you believe in the law of karma? Do you know how to be free from the law of karma?" The key questions had been adapted by permission to fit the culture.

The week of the seminar was remembered for a horrific tragedy. A propane tanker truck had overturned and caught fire on a busy intersection in Bangkok. Within minutes fire engulfed a large area, burning 85 people to death and injuring over 100 more. Some 47 vehicles were burned down to bare metal. It looked like a war zone. Only twenty minutes before the tragedy my taxi had passed that very area. Four of my missionary colleagues escaped death by only two car lengths. God had given us protection and safety. It was an extremely sobering event.

After surveying the Nong Khaam District we began methodically distributing Gospel tracts to every house. There was much prayer before, during and after the distribution to the 18,000 homes. One day we received a phone call in response to the tract. "What does it mean, 'Come to me'? Who said that? Could you come to our house and explain it?" I jumped at the chance. An invitation to a home was a rare opportunity for us as complete strangers. I took along a new Christian who I was discipling. We easily found the home just within walking distance from the two story townhouse we used for church worship and meetings.

Five women sat expectantly in a semi-circle on the floor as we entered the three room house. I began explaining the Gospel carefully beginning as usual with creation and progressing on to the life of Christ. After a couple hours of witnessing and answering their questions they said very earnestly, "We all want to become Christians." I was dumbfounded. Surely they didn't fully understand what they were committing themselves to after just one hearing! I didn't know that they had heard some of the Gospel before.

The new Christian with me shared a short testimony, and then we left literature and I prayed for them. I promised that I would be back the next week with the Christian worker to explain it better.

The following Sunday the worker and I arrived to find the same family eagerly awaiting our arrival. My colleague went through the Gospel just as I had done, even using some of the same illustrations. They were adamant—they wanted to accept Christ. She led them in prayer—Grandma aged 80, Mother aged 57, and three adult daughters were born into God's kingdom. Immediately they wanted to take down the idol shelf. No, we cautioned—just wait. They had a brother who lived with them. We had not met him and it was still his religion. We did not want to upset him. We merely prayed in the name of Jesus to invalidate any evil powers present and claimed the blood of Jesus for their protection.

"Joy," the mother began, "since you prayed for us last week my knees were healed." I was perplexed. I had not prayed for her knees. It must have been her faith! We promised to return on Tuesday.

That day when we came to teach them we met the son. "Tell me what to do. How do I become a Christian? My sister wakes me up at 3:00 a.m. to tell me about Jesus. What do I do?" he blurted out as he was wringing his hands.

"Yes, tell him the story, the *whole* story. We love hearing it," the sisters chimed in. So for the third time in ten days we were telling them the Gospel in full detail. The son was ready to pray. He took off his Buddhist amulet from his neck and held it between his hands in a worship pose before the idol shelf. "What are you doing?" asked an astonished sister.

"I'm saying goodbye to my old religion," he shot back. A whole family of six adults had come into the kingdom of God largely through one Gospel tract.

"Joy, did you say that God is everywhere?" the mother asked. "Yes," I said. "Well yesterday I was going to work when the bus broke down. I didn't want to be late and thought that if God is everywhere maybe He could help. I prayed. And all the sudden the bus started and the driver didn't know why. Do you think that was God?" As a brand new Christian she was personally experiencing God's power.

We went daily to teach this spiritually hungry family. By Saturday they said, "We usually work on Sundays and get overtime pay at the factory. But we have decided we won't work tomorrow. We are going to church to tell God that we are His new children." They never did go back to work on Sundays, but always came to church.

With the addition of this family our Sunday attendance reached 29 and we were overcrowded in our meeting place. We found a new location and moved into a three story store front across the highway, near this family's home. Here we could accommodate about 60 worshippers.

About a year later the grandmother died. We had been preparing for the inevitable so jumped into action the morning the call came. We discovered that Grandma had no birth certificate so officially she did not exist. Yet in death she had to have a death certificate to be buried or cremated. The family was financially limited and so decided on a cremation. The community headman had to come to verify her death so a certificate could be issued. Then church people helped with the arrangements.

As we sat around on the floor of their home for the funeral service we were all startled to see the son appear from the bedroom wearing a bright red shirt! By Thai custom, mourners, particularly the immediate family, wear black. "Grandma isn't dead. She's alive with Jesus," he explained.

By evening the same day we had moved the body directly to the prearranged temple crematorium. Expediency was needed since Thai have beliefs that a dead body may leave a house haunted. Their home was rented as was our house and the church building, so we had nowhere to retain the body.

This family became active in the Nong Khaam church. The son played the guitar for worship services and his sister played the electric organ. Another sister counted the offerings and the mother prepared communion trays. God once again proved His Word that it would be fruitful.

With only one other church in the whole district, this was quite literally virgin territory for the Gospel. It was an area of many factories, including Buddhist image molding. About this time a group of Christians from a church in Oregon had a burden for Thailand and came to do prayer walks in the capital city. We invited them to come to our part of town for a prayer walk too.

We prayed together for guidance and protection and then split into two teams to traverse separate routes. As we walked along praying quietly God brought to our minds powers to be bound as we passed various shrines. The team I was with was on a path I often took to church. Suddenly, out of seemingly nowhere, an angry burly man stepped out and began speaking in broken English. "Where you from?" he asked one of our male guests.

"America," was the simple reply.

"I hate America! I hate George Bush! I love Saddam Hussein!" he bellowed repeatedly as he shook his fist inches from our guests' noses. We never broke pace nor stopped praying as he followed us for a block yelling his fury. We realized that was a spirit we had neglected to bind. It was totally unprovoked and we recognized it for what it was, spiritual warfare. I had never seen the man before and never did again although I walked there regularly.

It impressed on me the continuous need for the spiritual armor of Ephesians six. I began a practice I have observed daily ever since. When I first awaken in the morning I conscientiously pray on the Christian's armor piece by piece. Invariably, when I get to the shoes I sense a physical peace settle over me. "Thank you, Lord, for the shoes. I put on the shoes of the preparation of the Gospel of Peace. Help me to think peace, speak peace and live out peace today for You are the Prince of Peace who reigns within me."

To me learning to minister in the city was really no different from in the rural areas. The enemy was the same. God proved that He was the same as well—sufficient to meet every problem and need.

It was the middle of my term but I was being asked to go on missionary tour—in Australia. It was just the change of pace I needed. Using my days off and some vacation time I managed to have all the messages, slides and slide script ready. Everything had to be prepared from scratch since all my tour material was in storage in California!

I was assigned to start in Western Australia, and in seven weeks work my way across to Sydney on the other coast. My most challenging commitment was in the first week when I was scheduled to address the local Rotary Club. I knew I could not share the Gospel directly, but maybe there was an indirect way. I was praying with friends when the Lord gave us just the right title and theme, "Investing Your Life in a Worthy Cause." It was perfect. I told the governor's story and what he said in witnessing to his upper class friends.

On the eight hour train ride to Kalgoorlie, a major gold mining town in Western Australia, I passed through tens of miles of nothing but brush, not even litter— apparently no one lived there. I was especially struck that in the vast barrenness *God* was there. On the trip I discovered in a local newspaper that I would be speaking to a ladies' group composed of nominal Christian society ladies, Alliance women and aboriginal women. I wondered how I could communicate to such a spectrum. Again the Lord was faithful to give the right message.

One morning it occurred to me—*this was the fulfillment of my Bible college dreams.* My MK roommate had grown up in this very area and the aborigines remembered her. Nearly 30 years before, my roommate and I had talked of crewing on a ship to visit Australia.

In Melbourne to the south I discovered the Aussie "op shops" (known to Americans as thrift shops) and was thankful to find some warm clothes unavailable in Thailand. September was spring in the southern hemisphere but I was quite cold being more accustomed to year around tropical temperatures. The good used apparel was easily disposed of when I left the continent to return to Asia.

In the Spanish church near Melbourne I met Liz, a promising college student and Peruvian pastor's daughter whose family had immigrated to Australia. I urged her to visit me in Thailand. It took seven years before she finally took me up on the invitation and came as our first Australian Alliance Youth Corps participant to Bangkok. She later taught for a year in the Dalat School in Penang.

Traveling by train and bus to Canberra, the capital of Australia, I happened to meet a young lady lawyer who was a missionary candidate in another organization. We began corresponding and four years later she was the one to introduce me to a Thai student from Khonkaen, where I had lived. It was as though God had a network of divine appointments for me all over the world. Some of my most faithful prayer supporters came out of my first Australian tour.

Back in Bangkok I continued where I had left off two months earlier, using friendship evangelism among the methods of winning people to Christ. For three years we had witnessed to our neighbors in word and life style. I had purposely taken the garbage out to the trash can on the lane in the evenings when other neighbors were likely to be heading for the same disposal unit. It gave a natural chance to build relationships and assured them we were human too—we had garbage!

At New Year's we took literature gift packets along with homemade chocolate cake or sweet rolls to the neighbors and acquaintances. This was the normal gift giving time in the local culture and the Gospel was easily received in that season. I felt we had built relationships and we had earned a hearing.

In Sisaket I had tried having a small evangelistic birthday celebration for my 40th birthday. My neighbors saw no significance in the American big 4-0. In fact, they thought it strange! I had been culturally irrelevant. I had decided then I would try again for my 48th—the fourth cycle birthday. Multiples of 12 years beginning at the fourth cycle or 48th year were considered worthy of note in Thai culture. I was now approaching my 48th birthday.

I arranged for a catered buffet dinner to be served in our voluminous main floor. We borrowed folding chairs from the church. I arranged for special music and a sermonette by a childhood friend who was now a Thai hospital chaplain in Bangkok. I gave a short verbal testimony of God's care for me in 48 years and why I came to Thailand. I then distributed my written testimony on an attractive church bulletin.

It was entitled: *My Answer*

Many times I am asked by Thai people, "How long have you lived in Thailand? What do you do here?" I would answer that I had come as a child with my father and my mother after the Second World War.

"Then you must love Thailand?"

"Yes, I love Thai people," I would respond.

Sometimes people would continue, "You must have a lot of personal merit since you've lived in Thailand for tens of years offering up your life to help people."

But I would answer, "Not at all. I don't consider myself to have any merit at all. Even though I have spent more than 30 years in Thailand already; I've worked as a nurse assisting hundreds of patients; as a religious teacher I've counseled and taught thousands of people. Even my profession, my education and my experience all have no value. They are a zero in the sight of God who is the Creator of the world. Because God said that our righteousness (or what man would count as all the personal merit) is nothing but filthy rags or old cloths soiled with car grease. There is no use for them at all. They must be discarded........."

The God who created the world created man as a holy be-ing but man sinned....I will tell you from my experience how Jesus now lives enthroned in my life.....I know my date of birth but I do not know my date of death—that second when I take my last breath. The same goes for everyone else on earth. But I have no worry or question what will happen to me when I die. I know for sure that I will go stay in heaven with Jesus.

God has stated that every person has only one appointed time to die. Following that he will be judged by God....I have no fear of that judgment.

I am happy to be one of your friends today but I have a condition. I can only be your friend in this life in the world. Whenever I die that is the end of our friendship unless you invite Jesus to cleanse you of sin. Then we can be friends in the next life in heaven forever.

So this is the reason I have come to Thailand to share good things with many, many people....I have happiness, peace and satisfaction. I desire that Thai people may have the same.

Joy Boese

May, 1993

In keeping with the local custom for a special event I gave out "Joy" brand souvenir pens and scripture note pads to all the guests. We had borrowed a TV and a VCR from a church member. I turned on parts of the *Jesus* video while we ate and during the odd moments of the evening. At the end of the evening I said, "If anyone would like to borrow a *Jesus* video I have two copies available." Eight families signed up. And we began passing the video from home to home.

About a month after my evangelistic birthday party a video had been returned to me. It was time to give it to the neighbors across the street. This family had observed our every move. They knew who got up early and when we went to bed. They had seen who came and went in our house. They had seen the good and the bad. Friday night when I rang their doorbell, the adult son answered the gate but his eyes were red from crying. His 62 year old mother had had a stroke and was partially paralyzed. A relative had swindled him of a large amount of money, and he was losing the house; nothing was going right. I thought to myself, *This is not the time to give him the video.* But here I was. So I handed it to him.

Sunday morning it was *my* doorbell that was ringing. The neighbor man was there saying, "Come quickly, my mother wants to enter the Jesus way *now.*" I was dumbfounded and mumbled, "Well, uh, has she seen the *Jesus* video yet?"

"She is looking at it this very moment. She doesn't want to wait. Please come now."

I yelled up the stairs to my coworkers, "Hey, you guys, pray! The neighbor lady wants to accept the Lord."

I walked across the narrow lane and into their living room. I had never seen anyone so prepared to receive Christ. Grandma was sitting on her couch-bed with her hands raised in a prayer-worship position. Tears were streaming down her cheeks as she watched the *Jesus* video. "I want to enter the Jesus way," she said. "I have followed the Buddhist path for 60 years and look what it has gotten me...nothing. I want to follow Jesus now."

I did not need to open my Bible because the scripture was coming from the TV. Jesus was giving the Sermon on the Mount: Ask and it will be given to you (Matthew 7:7). I prayed with Grandma and said, "I'll be back this afternoon to tell you more. I have to go and teach Sunday School now."

When I returned in the afternoon she was smiling. "Will you cut these spirit strings off my wrists?" she asked. No one had taught her. The Holy Spirit was already at work revealing the incompatibility of her new found faith with those shabby cotton strings worn to ward off evil.

It was not difficult to follow up and teach her every day since she lived so close. I usually chose evenings when her son and his wife and their two children would be home to hear the lessons. One day when I came to teach the family, the son informed me, "We are all Christians now. We bought cross necklaces. See?" and he held out his show piece for my inspection. I suggested we should talk to Jesus about it and ask Him to enter each one's heart and cleanse of sin. They readily agreed.

For some reason neither I nor my coworkers felt led to invite them to church. Maybe it was because Grandma's partial paralysis would leave her out. How could she climb the stairs to our second floor meeting room? Maybe it was because we feared for the son to meet a fringe church member who lived nearby and was a problem drinker. He could be a stumbling block. We just continued a weekly Bible Study.

Then one evening the son announced, "We are going to church on Sunday."

"You are? Do you know where the church is?" I replied in surprise.

151

He responded in the negative and we gave directions. Sure enough the family came—even Grandma. She had to be carried up the stairs. But she sat there beaming. She had read the entire New Testament by faithfully reading a portion every day. Later the Lord was pleased to heal Grandma of her paralysis and she was able to walk up the stairs to church by herself. The family members were baptized and attended church regularly. In a round-about way it was a birthday party that loosened the latch on this family's hearts. Friendship evangelism had won this family to Christ.

I lay down on the cool tile floor of the Alliance Guest Home bedroom and cried in self pity. I was hot, exhausted and thirsty. I had just finished moving all the mission furniture and my personal belongings from my home of four years to the mission storage rooms. For the third time in my missionary career I was the last one to move out of a house that had been shared by three or more single girls. Each had left this or that unwanted item behind. Now I had supervised a half dozen workers in loading and unloading two ten-wheel trucks and navigated across Bangkok in paralyzing traffic. It was the hot season and the promised helpers had not materialized. But that was not the whole problem. Somehow I had allowed old busy habits to creep in. I had neglected to process all my emotions. My little vessel was in danger of sinking if I didn't unload soon.

It had been a tough term in spite of the excitement of families coming to Christ and seeing a church take shape. I had served on the field leadership team for four consecutive years and carried some heavy confidential burdens. Then there were record numbers of missionary retirements and resignations. In a close-knit missionary family these felt like deaths and I had not allowed myself time to grieve. I was *more* than ready for a rest!

At my medical examination I had learned that my severe headaches were from an age related spinal degeneration. I was advised not to carry or lift anything weighing more than five or ten pounds. Otherwise the nerve would be pinched and I could count on a headache for at least 24 hours. I wondered how I would manage my heavy suitcases alone on the trip home to the States. I looked perfectly healthy and capable and would be expected to lift my suitcases up for the U.S. customs inspection in Los Angeles. I had a plan.

I went to the local hospital and asked to buy a soft ortho-pedic collar. I explained I was having a 30 hour trip across the ocean and wanted the neck support. Without so much as a glimpse of me a doctor wrote an order and I purchased my collar. It was a tremendous aid for resting on the plane. And in Los Angeles it did the trick. Wearing the soft collar made me appear "disabled" and a kind male passenger lifted my baggage for me!

For the first two weeks home I did little more than sleep and get up to eat. So out of character was it that my mother asked my sister if I could possibly be on drugs? I could hardly wait to get to the national office in Colorado Springs and unload some hurts. They too were grieving over some issues and could empathize. They readily agreed to my request for some Christian counseling to assist in recovery.

Then I found that God had a special treat for me. I had usually lived with my parents or friends each furlough. This time I had a distinct need for a place of my own. Perhaps it was the rigors of adjusting and flexing to five personalities under one roof during the past term. Or perhaps it was simply my age. The mission board had a housing rental allowance of $500 a month during home assignment. In spite of the plentiful vacant housing in California, I could find nothing within the budget. Then I spotted a small ad in the local newspaper. It was for senior citizen housing at $432 a month. Phoning the manager I asked if you had to be senior to rent. "Yes, 55 and over," was the immediate reply.

"Oh, I'm only 49," I answered disappointedly.

"Well, do you have a steady job?" The question took me by surprise. I had never really considered missionary work as a job before.

"Well, yeah. I'm a missionary home on furlough from Thailand for one year," I said, a bit unsure if that qualified.

"Oh, we love missionaries. Can I send you a brochure?"

Reading the literature I felt in my heart this was it. The town was half way between my parents' city and where my sister lived. The apartment was on the bus line. Shopping centers, supermarkets, post office and fast food were all within walking distance. An added benefit was a Thai restaurant within the block. The apartment was furnished with refrigerator and stove. The clubhouse had a laundromat. There was even a swimming pool. I could not have imagined such a marvelous treat.

By borrowing extra furniture from my parents and sister I had all my needs met. The Alliance Women opened the district supply cupboards and I was generously provided all the linens, dishes and appliances I needed. It was like a wedding shower and Christmas combined.

Several days after signing the year's contract the manager quietly requested, "Joy, don't tell anyone here how old you are. I wasn't supposed to let you rent."

"Well, this is God's answer to my need," I replied happily. The solitude gave ample opportunity to recuperate and get back on track with a balanced lifestyle once again.

One day while I was in the swimming pool I noticed an Indonesian-looking resident walk past in a familiar blouse. I called out to her, "Excuse me, is your blouse from Thailand?"

Her face lit up, "Yes, and I'm from Thailand too." I spoke to her in Thai and she was so flabbergasted she almost fell into the pool. For 15 minutes I fielded a barrage of questions. She peppered me with queries, hardly waiting or hearing the answers. Getting chilled in the pool I invited her up to my apartment to continue the conversation. Without hesitation she followed me. An hour later I still had not had a chance to change from my swimsuit.

My new friend was the daughter of the founding doctor of Sisaket Provincial Hospital. We discovered we had many mutual friends in that town. She had come to America to teach and she had lived and worked in a number of states. At this particular moment God had brought me to the very apartment where she was. Although a devout Buddhist she attended church with our family on occasion and enjoyed a special Easter drama with us. Later in Thailand I visited her elderly mother several times.

I soon found that these apartments were my mission field. Lonely people with time on their hands were ready to talk. A couple of backslidden Christians began attending church again. I was known as "the little missionary lady." I had several meaningful conversations with a homeless man living on the street near the supermarket. The Spanish cobbler in the shopping plaza and Sri Lankan hairdresser also were open to a witness. For four years at a time in Thailand I had been the alien and stared at. Now I had a whole year to be an American in my own country. It was wonderful to walk down the street and to be a nobody. I was walking on the ground instead of standing on a pedestal.

During my fall and spring missionary tour assignments I was humbled repeatedly having to ask for help to lift my suitcase. Sometimes a frail widow or an elderly host carried my bags. I had prayer for healing on several occasions, but it was not yet God's time to release me of the physical infirmity of my neck. However in August, 1998, I knew God was ready to touch me. When I was anointed and prayed for at our annual mission retreat I was instantly healed. Lifting a 50 pound suitcase no longer caused pain in my neck.

At the end of the home assignment year I was ready for another term of overseas service. I had gotten a second wind and now could continue the marathon.

23—Bangkok

"My people will live in peaceful dwelling places, in secure homes, in undisturbed places of rest." Isaiah 32:18 had been impressed on me as a promise from the Lord for my sixth term. The house in Nong Khaam District the last term had been just what we needed for ministry, but it was far from a haven of rest. The motorcycles whizzing by day and night deafened us. Telephone callers would frequently ask, "Are you on a public telephone on the sidewalk?"

"No, this is the quietest place in the house," I would say apologetically.

The Lord had provided so wonderfully on home assignment, I expected He would do the same for this new term. "Lord, where are my neighbors? Then I'll know where to look for a house." Within the first week I met my friend, the hairdresser.

"Where are you going to live this term?" she inquired.

"Right here in the area of our mission office," I replied.

"Well, do you have a house yet?"

"No."

"I know just the house for you!" she exclaimed. We walked the five minutes together across the street to a three story shop house and had a look. I felt in my heart that this was it. I was impressed with the wallpaper and parquet floors. I had never had it so good before. I walked around to the neighbors to see who they might be.

"Is it quiet at night here?" I asked one housewife.

"Yes, there are just a couple of pubs and a gay bar here," she answered. That was quite normal for this part of Bangkok and really could not be avoided.

The church I was assigned to had plenty of missionary personnel but few Thai leaders. Worship was attended by 200 people on Sunday afternoons at facilities rented from the English-speaking Evangelical Church of Bangkok. I felt very boxed in—

we were limited in space, parking, Sunday School rooms and schedule. The team joked, "Keep your schedule written in pencil because it will likely change." And change it did. Our part-time senior pastor was full time director of the Bangkok Bible College and he wore many other hats besides. If the college or another organization scheduled an event, then we had to change our church schedule to fit. It all seemed backwards to me.

My joy in ministry was derived from visiting neighbors and witnessing to taxi drivers. Personal evangelism, teaching an adult Sunday School class and one-on-one discipleship filled my time. Then came an announcement of a cell church seminar to be held in Bangkok. Three of us team members requested permission to go and learn what we could to enhance our church's small home groups. It was the beginning of a wave of change.

What we learned fit the need in our church. Furthermore, Trinity Church in Singapore was willing to send a pastor to hold a similar seminar for our church. Within a month we had all arrangements made and 50 participants eager to learn. Training materials were hot off the press and there was an air of excitement. The only drawback was that our senior pastor was still only part time.

Two and a half months later in February, 1996 the unbelievable happened. All 13 missionaries and Thai staff were in Singapore to attend two cell church seminars and visit functioning cells. Suddenly we said, "What have we done? We've left the entire church with just the secretary all week!" But the whole team caught the vision and a special bonding resulted. There was a fresh impetus for our Bangkok cell groups.

About mid year I again entered a parenthesis of ministry. Unexpectedly the Australian C&MA needed a missionary for tour ministries for seven weeks. Having toured there in 1992 I was the logical one to go on short notice. Furthermore, my brother's family, who were missionaries to the Philippines, would be home in Australia for the birth of a child. I would be in the right place at the right time to enjoy a new nephew. It would be a real treat after missing so many special family events through the years.

At 9 p.m. on a Wednesday the church secretary and I were sharing a taxi home from prayer meeting across town in Bangkok. We were stopped at the last intersection from home, waiting for the traffic light to change. Tires screeched behind us and, "Bang! Bang!" we were jolted by a vehicle in the darkness. It hit us so hard that it bounced and hit us a second time.

"In the name of Jesus we claim healing of every part of our bodies," I blurted out, hardly even thinking. *I can still go to Australia with two broken legs,* was my next thought. My departure was only ten days away.

The jolt knocked the taxi meter box out of the dashboard and to the floor. Our seat was shoved into the front seats. "Are you all right?" asked the driver.

"Yes, just give us five minutes to calm down," we replied. We had to climb over the front seat to get out. Walking around to the rear we were shocked to find the taxi was essentially totaled. The entire back section was smashed—the propane tank shoved under what had been the back seat where we had been sitting. We thanked the Lord for His protection and walked the five minutes home in the darkness.

Miraculously we sustained no whiplash or broken bones, only bumped shins. As I sat in my easy chair, ice packs on my knees, I recalled the last request in prayer meeting less than a half hour before. "And pray for the protection of missionaries as they travel in our country." God had answered.

Then it was that I realized—that was a propane gas tank that had been hit. It didn't explode on impact! Later the field director said, "Always jump out immediately if you are hit from behind as the tank is likely to explode into flames." We had sat there, ignorant of the danger, for a full five minutes. The Holy Spirit reminded me of Jeremiah 5:22 where the sand is a boundary set by God, the waves can go no further. It was as if God had placed His hand upon us—danger could come only so far and no further.

Bangkok traffic seemed to be getting worse by the day. One Wednesday afternoon I decided I would try walking to church. The secretary also wanting the exercise and a challenge, joined me. Traffic hardly moved. Hordes of sweaty people jostled across pedestrian bridges and crowded sidewalks. We timed it— less than two hours. One time the same route had taken me three and a half hours by taxi. We now knew that should it be necessary, we could walk and how long it would take. It was a comforting thought in such unpredictable traffic.

Normally I rode the minibus with its video, telephone, newspapers and magazines. It was cooler than an air conditioned taxi, only one-fifth of the price, and the only bus line that refused to take on passengers when every seat was occupied. Other buses packed humans in like sardines. I always allowed an extra hour for travel. I had decided there was no use to complain about the traffic. It would not change anything. That is what all the non-Christians did anyhow. If I complained I would be no different from them. So I chose to use the time in redemptive ways--reading my magazines and writing letters.

Once I boarded a bus and traffic just inched along. In an hour and a half we had traveled only a mile. For 40 minutes we had stopped still. The bus driver actually fell asleep at the wheel. We had to awaken him to open the door for a passenger who decided to get off and walk. Bangkok had to be the only place in the world where a driver could sleep at the wheel in mid-traffic for 40 minutes and not hurt a flea! A bus ticket checker sat ahead of me obviously bored. I handed her a Gospel tract. She was delighted. "Do you have a Bible or New Testament I can have?" she asked. She was a new Christian. I never did make it to the church; I had to turn around and return home. But I was not disappointed. I knew that God's appointment for me that night was not prayer meeting, but the contact with the ticket checker.

Every October we seemed to experience extra heavy spiritual warfare. It seemed that every major religion had a celebration. The end of Buddhist Lent, a Chinese vegetarian observance, a Hindu festival and even western Halloween vied for space on the calendar. The death of venerated King Chulalongkorn was commemorated annually on October 23. The evangelical churches regularly chose a week during school holidays in October to hold revival and praise meetings. The resulting conflict in the heavenlies was almost palpable.

Then on October 24, 1995 we witnessed a total solar eclipse. The local people attributed eclipses to the phenomenon of a frog eating the moon. They made offerings of nine black items including black chicken and black coffee. A neighbor exhorted me that day to tap all my potted plants to ensure that they would

160

flower. Needless to say, I left her advice unheeded—besides, my plants were not the flowering type!

The following October, radio, TV and paper flyers announced that a well known fortune teller had divined that 3,000 people whose first names began with the letter "S" would die. This curse of death could be averted however by an offering of bananas. Within the week all over the city hands of golden bananas could be seen hanging on fences or perched on walls. Incense sticks were stuck into the flesh of the fruit and a penned note stated "There is no one in this house by name of S." As I walked past neighbors' homes each day I saw these bananas blacken and rot. My heart cried out, *Lord deliver them from fear!* Besides that, it was my favorite kind of banana they were using! (Predictably the price of bananas went up and then the markets ran out of stock.)

Walking home from the bus stop one afternoon I was ready to enter my lane when a lone motorcyclist approached me. The road was empty and I thought it odd he needed to pass so close to me. Then there was a jerk and he sped away. Suddenly it hit me—he was a purse snatcher! He managed to tear away only one strap as I had a secure grasp on my bag. Indignant but thankful, I blurted out to my neighbors who were seated around the corner from the street. "A motorcyclist tried to snatch my purse. But look! God protected me and the man only got a strap."

They vocalized their surprise adding, "And you didn't even have a necklace on."

"I never wear jewelry on public transportation or on the street. I don't want to attract the attention of would-be thieves," I explained. I was sure that somewhere a prayer partner had prayed for my protection.

One of the first things I did when I returned to Thailand was to make contact with all my various acquaintances—Auntie S the fortune teller in Sisaket, the families in Nong Khaam District and the ex-governor who was wasting away with a rare degenerative disease. I discovered that he had been on a respirator in a private ICU room for seven months while I was in America.

When I went to visit him, I was alarmed by his wife's emotional state. She was nearly burned out supervising his 24 hour

161

care. She carried on a pediatric practice and then was at his side from noon until midnight daily. It was sad to see such a powerful man as a helpless invalid. His wife had become an expert lip reader and translated his conversations for his visitors. Every two or three months I took the one day trip by bus to go for a couple hours' visit and return to Bangkok. When he was still a governor everyone wanted to visit him. Now when he no longer had a title, it seemed everyone was too busy to care. Whenever possible I took a new guest or a church member along to visit.

Once when I had the governor on my mind all day I phoned to see how he was. I discovered his wife was away in Bangkok at the funeral of the governor's father. Knowing the strong anti-Christian feelings of the family I recognized it as an opportune time to express real Christian love. Miraculously, I was able to locate his family and find out at which temple the body was. I was quite unfamiliar with that part of town, but God's appointment was obvious since I found it quickly.

The only sibling I had met previously was the younger brother who had attended the governor's baptism. Two of the five sisters, and two brothers were extremely religious. They told me that they chanted Buddhist prayers every morning at 5:00 for their governor brother to revert to Buddhism. I told them that since he could not be there for his father's funeral, I wanted to be the representative. I snapped photos and chatted with each one, building a relationship so I could make a home visit later. At the end of the week I was able to go and visit the governor and tell him of his sisters' friendly acceptance of me as a Christian. A door had been opened.

A month later I went to visit the three sisters. I intended to merely continue building the relationship and not to talk about religion. To my surprise, that was all they wanted to talk about. They shared their strict Buddhist observance and then asked point blank, "Now what does Christianity teach? Please tell us. You have listened to us. We want to hear you." I had earned a hearing. How fantastic of God to give such an opportunity!

Throughout the four year term I continued visiting the governor until furlough. His brother was promoted to a full governorship. I met a third brother one day while I was visiting.

Otherwise nothing changed for the four and a half years that he lay in the ICU bed. How I grieved for him.

One day a letter came from my sister, Carol, in Hong Kong where she and her family were living. She wrote that she had met a woman who knew me from the Buddhist temple. I did not recognize the name. Then Sue herself wrote to me that we had met in the temple in Ubon in 1983. She was investigating Buddhism at that time, and she had been warned by the western abbot, "Just be careful of the missionary lady." The very day she had gone to the temple was the very same day I happened to be there too.

"You'll never truly be satisfied until you find Jesus because He is the Way," I had told her. The Holy Spirit used God's Word to put her under such conviction she could not sleep for three days and three nights. Nevertheless she went back to England and ordained as a Buddhist nun for seven and a half years. She saw a film on Christian work in Hong Kong. It was on the power of the Holy Spirit to release drug addicts. Sue realized *that* was what she wanted. She left her Buddhist robes and accepted Christ.

For the next five and a half years as a Christian she grew and kept in contact with former Buddhist friends. One day a couple of western monks on a pilgrimage came by and she invited them for breakfast. Two elderly lady prayer partners were also summoned to the breakfast. Much to her dismay the monks would not listen to Sue's witness. However, one of the ladies got up from the breakfast table and brought a basin of warm water and began washing the monks' blistered feet. It was simply astonishing that they allowed her to do so. She was totally unaware that it was taboo for monks to be touched by a woman, and Sue made no move to tell her.

A couple weeks later this tangible love brought forth fruit. "I've met Jesus. What do I do—I'm still in Buddhist robes!" exclaimed a monk on the phone to Sue. And so the intercession of prayer partners many years before continued to bear fruit. Today Sue is in Christian ministry. For a while she worked with the drug addicts in Hong Kong but her heart has returned to Thailand.

About the middle of 1997 we began to see a distinct change in the spiritual atmosphere of Thailand that could only be attributed to God and to prayer. People were coming to Christ in our church every week—in the worship services, in home cell groups and through individual witness. I was asked to teach the baptismal candidates class on Sundays. I was thrilled and fascinated by the stories I was hearing.

A young woman who moved to Bangkok had some contact with a village church as a child. For ten years she wanted to become a Christian, but never met anyone who could tell her how. In a strange string of circumstances she received a Bible through a non-Christian friend and ended up in our church. The moment she walked into the sanctuary and saw the large wooden cross at the front she knew. This is it—*this is what I have been looking for!* When the invitation was given, she accepted Christ in her heart.

That week she witnessed to fellow employees and one accepted Jesus. Her zealous witness brought others to Christ. By the time she finished all her discipleship lessons and pre-baptism classes, she was a fluent mini-evangelist. She invited her boss to come to her baptism. He came with his wife, his mother and his eleven year old daughter. All three generations accepted Christ, were discipled together and were eventually baptized. The boss became church camp director two years later. The eleven year old started winning her playmates to Christ. Then the original employee began Bible training to become a missionary.

Some baptism classes were as large as 22 members. There would be a lawyer sitting beside an uneducated house maid, an airline hostess beside a jeweler, a bar tender next to an insurance salesman, and college students next to an illiterate grandmother in her 70's.

The entertainment segment of society was becoming increasingly responsive spiritually. Miss Anchalee, the popular rock queen of Thailand, had come to Christ in 1989 and chosen our fellowship as her home church. She quietly blended in with regular church members in spite of her celebrity status. So unassuming was her presence that a visitor to church would overlook her among the guitarists accompanying the worship songs to the far left of the platform.

No doubt many had prayed for Anchalee's salvation through the years. One person was an American Peace Corps worker who lived in northeast Thailand during 1986-1987. Every

Saturday morning his Thai roommates were transfixed before the TV, watching Rock Queen Anchalee and other popular performers. He prayed regularly that God would bring the pop stars to salvation. He prayed for Christian song writers to emerge as well. Although Anchalee accepted Christ two years later, he did not hear how thoroughly God answered his prayers until ten years afterwards. Not only the Rock Queen herself, but many other entertainers met God. By 1998 a Christian song writer was busy composing pieces for her album.

A popular radio talk-show host chanced upon Dr. James Dobson's *Dare to Discipline* in her search for advice on how to raise her twin daughters. Finding references to the Bible she bought one, but could not understand it. She phoned Anchalee her fellow entertainer who invited her to church. When she was saved, her radio listeners marveled at her wise answers to their questions. They never guessed that she was quoting God's wisdom from His Word!

By the end of 1998 several Bangkok churches had joined together to put on a $50,000 TV show at prime time--11:15-12:15 at night. Most of the core personnel and film extras were our church members. Miss Thailand from the national beauty contest that year was a Christian and participated. There was a heavy outlay of time, energy and funds. But most of all there was worldwide prayer support among partners on five continents.

Bangkok churches, Christian organizations and missions volunteered the use of their telephones for the night of December 23. Volunteers were trained to man the phones, pagers and fax machines. The viewer response was overwhelming. By the time all the statistics were in, nearly 5,000 people had responded by machine or mail. It was indicative of a wave of spiritual hunger for truth. It was such a different world from the era of my childhood when the number of inquirers per month could all be counted on one hand!

There was a young doctor who was a devout Buddhist. During medical school he often ordained as a Buddhist monk for a month or two of school vacations. He meticulously followed all the rules but was perplexed by one thing. The renowned abbot who was his mentor often used the Bible for his discourses. *Why would this monk use the Christian's book?* he wondered. He began to investigate Christianity to see if the abbot was interpreting it correctly. He went along to church with some Christian friends to see for himself. When they tried to follow him up he objected. "I know where your church is and if I want to go, I will go myself. Just leave me alone. I am a devout Buddhist."

Later the doctor was intrigued by a fellow dermatologist in his department. The woman physician was a practicing Christian who had given most of her years to leprosy work. She was soon to retire and he asked her for Christian literature. He accepted her invitation to visit her church. It happened that it was a Sunday when baptismal candidates were sharing their testimonies. It was not long afterwards that the doctor accepted Christ. At his own baptism he officially changed his name to be "Dr. Met God." Patients would ask about his unusual name, "What god did you meet?" It was an immediate opportunity for him to share Christ with them.

In Thailand it is more important to attend a person's funeral than to go to a wedding. I could count at least 20 funerals, but only four weddings that I had attended in my four year term.

Normally for a Thai funeral everyone wears black. Buddhist funerals extend for an odd number of nights—three or five nights, or for very wealthy and highly honored persons there might be seven or nine nights. The priests chant each night. They are usually on a raised platform to the side of the coffin. A simple white cotton string is attached to the coffin and held by the seated monks to chant the deceased to the other world. There are incense sticks, candles and floral wreaths in abundance. Four monks hold up decorative fans with the inscriptions: (Death) is to go and not return. (Death) is to sleep and not awaken. There is no resurrection (from death). There is no escape (from death).

All during the ceremony the funeral guests sit respectfully with their hands clasped together in front of them in a worship posture. Afterwards there are the refreshments—fish soup, rice porridge or some Thai iced sweets.

As Christians we embraced the opportunity to go and be Christ's presence. To sit with the lone Christian family member looking helplessly on at the proceedings was the least we could do. But we always found chances to witness of God's love by action and usually in word. "What happens to Christians when they die?" someone would ask. This was just what we wanted them to ask, and the door was open to witness and give out Gospel tracts.

The custom in Thailand is to give a memento of the occasion, whether a funeral, a wedding or any special event. It could be a few cough drops wrapped in a handkerchief, a small booklet, or any item deemed appropriate to the occasion. One of our wealthy church members distributed videos of the *Jesus* film to all 300 guests at a church funeral. Scores of these were businessmen who would never enter a church building or attend any kind of evangelistic outreach. However, social obligation required their presence at the funeral of a valued customer's father or business associate.

It was at such a memorial service that I spoke with an elderly visitor at our church. I could tell by her apparel that she was from the rural areas. I asked her what province she was from.

"Prachinburi" she answered. My heart skipped a beat. I reached into my purse and pulled out a recent photo of my parents to show her.

"Did you ever know foreigners in that town who taught religion?" I asked.

"Oh, yes," she exclaimed, as she recognized the couple pictured. "Only they weren't wearing glasses then. The man showed slides about Jesus in my village. I well remember."

"Those were my parents," I said. "Mother and Dad were pioneer missionaries in that province in the 1950's."

This lady, Mrs. Somsee had borne five children. Her oldest son had gone away to work in another province many years ago but was never heard from again. Two other sons were addicted to drugs and drinking. A daughter went to Bangkok to further her education. Another daughter was a drug addict for 20 years. She left her four children with Mrs. Somsee, the grandmother. It was a very dismal family portrait to be sure. But there was one bright spot. The middle child had not only received an education in Bangkok, but she had found Christ as well. She had prayed for her family for ten years, but there seemed to be no interest. They were set in their Buddhist ways.

About six months after I first met Mrs. Somsee I heard that she was in the hospital with a foot infection. I took the interprovincial bus three hours' ride out of town. I was excited for the chance to go to my old hometown to visit. When we had lived there four decades earlier, there had been no hospital, no doctor, not even a nurse. Now there was a 30 bed hospital. The bus driver let me off directly in front of the hospital.

I found Mrs. Somsee quite easily and gave her a bag of oranges. After reading scripture and praying with her, I distributed Gospel tracts to the other patients on the ward. Returning to town I found I still had a couple of hours before my train was due. Outside the station an ice cream vendor called out hopefully, "Ice cream, Ma'am? Where are you going?" A foreigner in this little town was a rarity.

168

"Well, about 45 years ago my family and I lived in this town. We had a house near the railway station. I thought I would look for it," I answered.

"Oh, to the east, to the west," he sang out the opening lines of a Sunday School song. "Did your mother ever teach children here?"

"Why, yes," I replied.

"I was one of the little boys in her class," he said excitedly. "The meeting room was right over there." He pointed to a shop house behind him. "Here, look after my cart," he requested of a customer standing near by. "I'm going to take this lady to her old house." He then walked with me two blocks to the site.

There it was—much smaller than I had remembered it as a child. It was my spiritual birth place, where at the age of five I had accepted Christ. Though still standing, the house was in dire need of repairs. Neighboring tenants volunteered the information that it had been a lucky house. The last renters had won the lottery three times! As I walked around town other people remembered Mother's children's classes, Dad playing the trombone or Mother dispensing leprosy medicines.

In July of 1997 Thailand began to experience an economic crisis that plunged the country into a nose-dive. The currency was devalued by 50% and eventually 100%. Tens of thousands lost their jobs and by April of 1999 it was reported that two million of Thailand's 60 million people were unemployed. Rich people were selling their BMW's and private planes for half price. "Garage sales" sprouted in shopping mall parking lots as people sold their belongings from the trunks of their cars. The suicide rate soared and there was an overall pallor of hopelessness and desperation.

In the midst of this Mrs. Somsee came to Bangkok hoping to get money from her Christian daughter to care for her two adult children who were addicted to drugs and four grandchildren who were living with her. She was disappointed to find that her daughter and son had lost their jobs. That weekend was Mother's Day (celebrated on the Queen's birthday—August 12) when the churches usually plan a special outreach. Mrs. Somsee came along to church with her daughter. At the invitation to receive Christ she resolutely raised her hand. It had taken 46 years for the seed of the

Gospel to bear fruit in her heart. The next week she hopped on the back of a motorcycle taxi and dragged her son to church. Seeing the change in his mother, he too accepted Christ.

Mrs. Somsee was the only Christian in her small village of 200 homes and a large temple. The nearest Christian was an hour or two away. Her daughter and I traveled to the village to visit one day. We brought steamed sticky rice, barbecued chicken on a stick and bananas for a simple lunch together on the porch of her tumble-down house.

Mrs. Somsee had only a fourth grade education, and now with her poor eyesight could hardly read. I managed to teach her a discipleship lesson. In our church we used 12 lessons to disciple new Christians one-on-one and then six lessons in the pre-baptism class. I challenged her to ask God for a miracle to be able to read by herself. I shared the testimonies of other elderly Thai, such as an 80 year old man who had never been to school a day in his life. He could not read a single letter of the alphabet. When he became a Christian, he wanted to read the Bible. He prayed that God would write the alphabet on his brain. When he opened a Bible he could read it. But looking at a newspaper the words made no sense to him. God worked a miracle enabling him to read His Word! After sharing such stories with Mrs. Somsee I suggested that in the meantime she could have her oldest grandson read the Bible to her.

Our church was divided into four zones for pastoral care. Usually at Christmas, each zone would have a party. As the leader of the west zone, I suggested a Christmas outreach in the village. The members enthusiastically endorsed the idea. We prayed, planned and worked hard in preparation. We gathered clothes, dry goods, school uniforms, toys and books. Some non-Christian shop keepers gave us discounts for blankets and donated mosquito nets.

Then on a government holiday in December, 22 of us piled into vans and drove the two and half hours to the village. Upon our arrival we met nearly 60 children waiting impatiently at Mrs. Somsee's house.

Our team included three cell leaders who had been as-signed various responsibilities. Some ran a children's program with games and prizes. Others were on food detail and distribution of goods. We had a big supply of tracts and Christian literature.

We sang Christmas carols with guitar accompaniment. I had trained two members to tell the Christmas story to the children. Then everyone paired off and headed for village homes up dusty lanes to give out tracts and witness to people at home.

Mrs. Somsee was overwhelmed to experience so much love and attention. Like many elderly people, she had no birth certificate. She knew only that she was born the year of the goat in the twelve-year animal cycle popular with the older generation. I decided that December was as good a time as any and said, "Today is your birthday!" as I presented her with a cupcake and a candle. At age 75 it was her first birthday cake!

We had gifts for everyone. We did not want anyone to get the idea that we were buying Christians with material goods. We wanted to build good relationships with the neighbors. We gave Mrs. Somsee a large print Thai New Testament. The village headman had a TV and a VCR so we gave him a *Jesus* video. Likewise the school master got a *Jesus* video for the school and books for the library.

Although we had planned that this would be a witnessing time, God had a surprise for us. Mrs. Somsee's 41 year old son accepted Christ. His mind was disturbed by his drug addiction, but we noticed an immediate improvement in his behavior. God was at work in the village. It was an eye opener for our city Christians, and they enthusiastically agreed that it was better than the usual Christmas zone party back in Bangkok.

Distance made it impossible to really disciple Mrs. Somsee properly. But every time she came into Bangkok her daughter would phone me, "My mother is here." I would go and teach her another discipleship lesson. If she were in town for a week I would go every other day to teach her. By this time she could read. When the grandchildren went off to school every day she would take her New Testament to the back yard and sit under a tree to read for two hours. She finally finished the entire New Testament.

Mrs. Somsee told me how one day she sent the kids to school with no breakfast because she had nothing to feed them. "I asked God to forgive me because I knew they were hungry. I asked Him to please feed them. And that would be the day there would be a school lunch and the headmaster would send the leftovers home with the kids."

In June of 1998 I went to her village to see if she were ready for baptism. I gave her the train fare to come into Bangkok on the specified day. She told me how her rice supply was nearly gone. "I prayed to God, 'Jesus, when You were on earth You fed 5,000 people with only five hunks of bread and two little fishes. Could You make our rice last until we can get some more or have money to buy?'" The rice lasted and lasted as long as needed. God had heard His daughter's prayer of faith.

About the time I finished teaching that day it began to rain. I had taken two Alliance Youth Corps college kids with me to the village. They had been playing with the village children as I taught Mrs. Somsee. At the sound of the rain they came running for shelter on to the porch. They might as well have stayed outside. Her roof leaked so badly. She hurried around with little tin cans and bowls to catch the drips. I counted at least 30 leaks. The only dry spot was under my umbrella!

About this time the temple abbot began to miss Mrs. Somsee. For 60 years she had faithfully sat on the temple floor in the worship posture during the monks' chants. At first she had continued going to the temple as leftovers from the monks were given to the poor, and they gave generously to her. She had prayed, "Forgive me, Lord, for coming to the temple, but I have nothing to feed my family." But then she quit and decided as God's child He would take responsibility for her needs. She would trust God and not man.

"Haven't seen you lately," the temple abbot commented when she walked through the village one day.

"I'll tell you the truth. I have become a Christian," she answered respectfully.

"Good, it is a good way. Follow it closely," was his unexpected reply. The next week he gave her the monetary equivalent to ten village meals. Instead of thanking him she raised her hands to heaven and thanked God.

She came to Bangkok and I introduced her to the rest of the baptismal candidates. I was teaching a lesson on Jesus, our healer. Mrs. Somsee piped up, "Yes, that's right. I could not raise my arm as my shoulder was stiff and sore. So I put water on my hand and asked God to bless it for healing and rubbed it on my arm. And He healed it. See? I can raise my arm! Then I put water in my cupped hands and said 'God, please bless this water to heal my eyes' and washed my face with it. Now I can read my Bible." This little dried up wisp of a country lady was a real faith booster to the rest of the class.

In our church each quarter we baptized ten to twenty people. Due to time constraints, we allowed only three volunteers among the candidates to share three minute public testimonies each. It was always a great evangelistic event as non-Christian spouses, friends and relatives came to view the baptisms. The testimonies were a powerful witness and nearly always someone would be saved as a result.

In Mrs. Somsee's class we had 12 candidates. A lawyer zealously shared her testimony for 15 minutes. Then an architect enthusiastically testified for another 15 minutes. Only the jeweler stayed within his allotted three minutes. We were hopelessly overtime and into the second worship hour. But God is not easily boxed in by man's schedules. This was a very special occasion. We had two ladies aged 75 to be baptized that day. I knew that it was highly unlikely that they would ever again have opportunity to give a public testimony.

I quickly slipped up to the microphone, "Pastor, I know we are overtime but this is very special. I would like to interview these two women." There was an immediate murmur of approval across the audience and Pastor gave a nod.

"After 75 years in Buddhism what made you change?" Mrs. Somsee got started and I wondered if she would ever stop.

"In April when I returned to my village there was no water. The water jars were empty, the well was dry. There was not a drop to drink. The villagers had been chanting unsuccessfully for rain for four days." The local village custom is to take a gray cat and put it in a basket with a lid. The basket is marched around the temple and village while people chant for rain. Water is thrown on the cat by the villagers as it passes. It is punishment to the cat which has prevented the rain from falling because cats don't like getting wet.

Mrs. Somsee said she raised her hands in prayer to heaven as she ran around her own home several times petitioning the Lord for rain. Within a few minutes dark clouds gathered and a strong wind came up frightening her. "Not so strong, Lord. It's not wind we want, but rain!" At this the whole church burst out in gleeful laughter and applause. She turned to me, "Why are they laughing? I'm not through with the story yet!" The sky darkened and such a heavy rain poured down that all her water jars were filled. God had responded to her simple child-like faith.

Mrs. Somsee's oldest grandson finished grade six with high honors. God provided funds for him to attend a school in Bangkok. He began attending church with his aunt and in a few months accepted Christ at camp. Then he led his ten year old brother to the Lord. By November, less than one year from our Christmas outreach in his village, he was baptized. What a joy to see God bring three generations to Himself in one year—mother, son and grandson!

In January of 1999 my parents, Harvey and Grace Boese aged 82 and 78 years were privileged to visit Thailand again. We went to Mrs. Somsee's village. She was overjoyed to see those who first brought the Gospel to her village nearly 50 years before. Dad remembered using a kerosene lantern projector to show Gospel slides of the Life of Christ in some 70 or 80 villages during 1950's. Obviously this was one of the villages.

Mrs. Somee introduced us to her niece who had had a chronic skin disease something like eczema. No doctors or medicines had been able to cure it. When she talked to her aunt, Mrs. Somsee claimed God could heal it. So she agreed to have her aunt pray for her. "In the name of Jesus please, God, take this skin disease away. The doctors and all the medicines cannot help her. You have the power to heal. Thank you." The skin disease cleared up within a couple days. However it returned again. It cropped up when the niece went back to the Buddhist temple.

"See, you turned your back on God," the aunt scolded. The niece repented so Mrs. Somsee prayed again, "God, take it away completely. Don't let it come back again." She was once again healed.

She told us of another niece who at 45 years of age was dying of AIDS. The monks and sorcerers could not relieve the woman's pain with their chants and incantations. Mrs. Somsee snuck in after they left and quietly prayed for relief for her niece. "I didn't pray for healing because you cannot get well from AIDS," she said matter-of-factly. The woman slept soundly until ten o'clock in the morning. Then the family called for Mrs. Somsee to come again. Again prayer brought relief.

Yes, God was doing a new thing in Thailand. The seed of the Gospel was being sown through funerals, hospitalization, celebrations such as Mother's Day, Christmas and baptisms. The Gospel of John says that some plant and others reap the harvest. Mother and Dad were among those who had planted the Seed and now the Thai church was doing the reaping and all were rejoicing together.

I pulled an office email from my letterbox and stared at it. I did not know whether to laugh or cry. I was stunned. I was being asked to be the assistant field director for our Thailand Mission. I was computer illiterate, uncomfortable operating the office copy machine, and felt totally incompetent in the technical world of an office. On the other hand, I felt a strong sense that this was a solemn assignment from God. For six years I had been a reluctant member of the field leadership team. The Holy Spirit reminded me again that my gifts and my talents were not my own but God's. They were to be used for the good of all. It was a renewal of my call to intercession. I submitted to His will knowing He was the burden bearer. My simple reply was typed up on my old manual typewriter.

During the next two years I saw my ministry shift from management to leadership in both church and mission responsibilities. Our church was divided into four geographical zones for pastoral care. During the four year period that I was involved it had grown from 200 members to 350 members. I found myself the zone leader to 150 adults and children. The pastoral care was shared with the leaders of the five adult home cell groups and one children's cell. It was a challenge to stay a step ahead of my cell leaders anticipating what their leadership needs might be. Coaxing reluctant and insecure members to fulfill their leadership potential proved more difficult than providing resources for the eager leaders.

A young woman in my zone intrigued me. I felt drawn to her. Though a mature productive Christian, she was beset by a fiery temper that often caused her heartache and regret. I sensed a need for some deeper inner healing and mentoring. She was receptive of my offer to tutor her through a second level discipleship course that covered some basic inner healing. We met for several hours each week at my home and talked long hours on the phone. As her story unfolded, it was a testimony to God's faithfulness. Her name was L.

Thirty-six year old L had been raised in a traditional Chinese family in Bangkok. She was the ninth of eleven children. Her mother had tried to abort her as she had terminated three previous pregnancies. But L was too stubborn to be aborted. Her mother wanted to give her away as a toddler; but she was such a difficult child, they gave away her better-behaved sister instead. In Chinese culture, girls were considered of little value and none went to school.

In God's providence, the year that L turned eight coincided with the Prime Minister of Thailand's decree that all children eight years old and up *must* go to school. She soon loved to read. When most kids were spanked for not reading, she was disciplined for reading all the time and not working! Before she completed the sixth grade, however, she had to quit and help her mother sell goods. At age 16 she was sent to work in a cosmetics store.

One day she picked up a book someone had left half read. It was by a Korean pastor, Dr. Cho, on the gifts of the Holy Spirit. This was hardly a volume for a non-Christian. In the book was an illustration of a Christian woman's unforgiveness. The story put L under conviction as she had unforgiveness toward an older brother. She had thought herself a very good person. She religiously observed vegetarian rituals and did the right things. Now her refusal to forgive her brother had been pinpointed by the Holy Spirit as sin. She cried hard and decided she would become a Christian. A friend helped her find a Chinese church nearby.

L had a voracious appetite for spiritual truth. She devoured every Bible correspondence course available in one third of the time that it took most people to study. She memorized verses and gained a foundation in both the Old and New Testaments. She could not get enough of God and His Word. She found a church teaching Bible on Sunday afternoons and soon she was attending two churches on Sundays.

Four years after accepting Christ she felt called to study the Bible full time in a Bible School. However, she really did not fully qualify as she only had a fifth grade certificate. Her family also objected to her giving up her job. In Chinese-Thai families all unmarried children in the home turn over their pay checks to the parents. She had no money for school fees either. L gave God three conditions. If He was really calling her to Bible School He would need to (1) make her mother give permission for her to study (2) help L find sufficient income to meet her mother's needs as well as pay for L's schooling and (3) He must give her the brains to study!

It was a simple matter for God to handle. L got a part time job one day a week making shampoo and delivering it to sales representatives. The income was more than her former full time job and met her mother's expectation for income as well as her own need for school fees. Then her mother miraculously gave her permission to study even though she did not understand *what* it was she was going to study! Finally God gave her unusual understanding in her studies.

L had the highest average in her class and did not need to repeat a single course. One subject was a Greek language intensive that the professor said would be impossible for her to do since she had no high school diploma and no English language foundation. L begged to at least be allowed to audit it. The first day was a disaster—she took the assigned work home and cried to God that she could not understand any of it! The next morning when she looked at it everything made sense. In the class of 50 students with high school and college diplomas, she was one of the 20 who finished the course and even earned a B grade. God's wisdom enabled her to complete all studies on time. She was the only one in the class to complete a thesis and yet she could not be granted a degree because she had no high school diploma!

She wanted to study at the master's level to become a Bible professor but was told, "Go do your high school equivalency first so that you qualify. Then come back and we will talk."

While working full time she earned her high school equivalency in night school, and then a bachelor's degree at the university. All this time her mother and family, except for one older sister, had resisted the Gospel in spite of L's diligent prayers for them and zealous witness. L's youngest brother had scrambled his brains on drugs and attempted suicide twice. In 1996, he had jumped from a pedestrian bridge to the pavement below and crushed the back of his skull. The church had been very supportive of the family during his days in ICU. They literally prayed him back from death's door. L's oldest brother had a drinking problem and advanced tuberculosis. His wife and two children also lived with L and her mother. It was a very troubled and turbulent household in which anger and tempers flared routinely.

In March 1998 the doctor found that L's mother was going into a fast downward spin. Her kidneys were failing, and at age 72 she was given four months to live. L fasted and prayed. She begged the Lord to spare her mother's life until she would accept Christ. L took her mother to the ocean side for a few days and broke the news as frankly and as lovingly as she could. Her life was ending. Their financial status did not make dialysis an option. Even if it did, it would only buy a few months' time. Her mother was stunned. Ordinarily in Asia such information is withheld from a terminal patient. But L had a burden—she pleaded with her mother to accept Christ, before it would be too late. Her mother consented half-heartedly; but L didn't think it was a real commitment. They returned home to Bangkok with L making every effort to make life as pleasant as possible for her mother.

The next morning to L's amazement, her mother removed the ancestor shelf and family idols on her own initiative. She was finished with her old religion! L was delirious with joy and phoned the cell group leader requesting that the cell meet in her home that week. Her mother really understood only Chinese, but God had ordained that this particular cell was almost entirely of Chinese ancestry and could speak her dialect! As we sang worship songs and various ones shared in Chinese, it was quite evident that L's mother had made her choice to follow Jesus. I was the only one who didn't understand the language but the joy was visible on each one's face. One of the cell members quietly witnessed to the daughter-in-law and ended up leading her to Christ that night.

There were frequent prayer chain alerts for L's mother as she went through peaks and valleys physically. Church camp was coming up in May. The mother was insistent she wanted to go along. She had heard there were air conditioned rooms and in the midst of the hottest season of the year, she longed for some respite from the heat.

Camp seemed to be one big spiritual warfare that year. At times the prayer team felt overwhelmed. On the second night we nearly lost L's mother. The doctor and I were called out twice in the night to minister to her. The first time we thought her lungs were full of fluid. She was foaming at the mouth and incoherent in her speech. But the second time we realized we were dealing with a spiritual dimension as well. In her physically weakened state, demonic powers were attacking and trying to destroy her. We invoked the powerful name of Jesus. It quelled the storm and she stopped choking. Later we realized our camp was in the very province made infamous by the World War II Death Railway. Spirits of death, destruction and cursing were apparently still rampant. Furthermore a cult group had pitched 1,000 tents not long before us on this very camp site.

Three weeks later it was evident that L's mother could not last much longer. L was up day and night caring for her mother. The woman was restless and unable to eat. I was feeling quite drained being a moral support to L all this time. As zone leader my pastoral care included long hours on the phone as L cried and unburdened herself of multiple sorrows. Her sisters and brothers were very unsupportive. They said their mother's soul would be suspended in nowhere because after 70 years of good deeds she had disposed of her idols. Those gods would no longer help her. Her commitment to follow Jesus was only a few months old, so why would Jesus take her after death? The toxins in her blood were playing havoc and in her incoherent moments she said things that made L wonder if her mother really were saved.

But in her right mind, the frail woman repeated the only prayer she knew, "Thank you, Jesus. Thank you, Jesus." She affirmed her desire to be baptized even though she did not know exactly what it was, never having seen a baptism. The assistant pastor, a staff member and I made our way to the humble home one afternoon. In the presence of two daughters and a daughter-in-law, she was baptized by sprinkling as she lay on her cot. Everyone seemed relieved. The non Christians thought now Jesus would accept her. Two weeks later she passed peacefully into the arms of her Savior. The months of suffering had come to an end.

Amazingly the Buddhist family agreed to a Christian funeral. L's entire family attended the funeral meetings at church. Their hardness softened as Christians loved them and comforted them. On the third day before burial when the invitation was given to accept Christ, the oldest son raised his hand. It was a fulfillment of his mother's heart. Her first desire when she was saved was that this son would accept Christ.

L felt the loss of her mother keenly. She had prayed for her salvation for 17 years. One burden gone, she still had another. She had promised her mother that she would care for her youngest brother. For years already she had been the sole breadwinner for the mixed household. She began to seek the Lord's mind for her future. As I was mentoring her she shared her deep desire to go to seminary. At the October missions rally she had gone to the altar in tears—remembering that she had promised God that if He saved her mother she would serve Him full time. Now she was ready to make that promise good.

L spent a month praying and seeking God. In the midst of it Dr. John Stott of England was in Bangkok for lectures. He challenged his listeners, "Who will be the Timothys who will faithfully teach the Word of God to the next generation?" She remembered her original call to full time Bible teaching some 14 years before. She had gotten off track in a blur of studies and secular jobs. Now she wept and sobbed until a friend beside her said, "If you keep crying we are all going to be flooded out of the auditorium!" In her words, L said, "I realized God was inviting me once again to step into His plan." In stark faith she began applying to seminary.

In the meantime L's sister-in-law had been growing weak and had a bad cough. We suspected she had contracted tuberculosis from her husband, but she refused to go to the doctor. A week later she was dead, leaving two grade school children behind. It was a terrible shock to the family. Again they agreed to a Christian funeral. Since she died of tuberculosis, it was decided that she would be cremated. The only place for cremation in Thailand is in the Buddhist temple. We arranged to use the premises, but not involve any monks. Crematorium workers appeared very impersonal and mechanical as they handled several cases a day—except on Fridays. In the Thai language the word "Friday" literally translates as "day of happiness" so they never cremate on that day. One could not bring sorrow on a day of happiness they reasoned.

As we huddled around the funeral pyre L's family again heard the Gospel message. The assistant pastor packed the Gospel into a seven minute message as the temple hands impatiently waited to do their job.

A few months later L applied to the Bangkok Bible College and Seminary and was accepted as a graduate level student. She was exuberant returning from her final interview. But when she arrived home and found her youngest brother with drugs, her temper flared, "You know the doctor said you can't use drugs! You must take the doctor's medicine! I find the money to feed and clothe you and you don't even care!" He walked out of the house.

The next day he went away again without either of them saying a word to each other. That night she returned home late from teaching a Bible study. Wednesday morning in her devotions God spoke to her from Psalm 107. He would release her from her burdens. She puzzled, "I don't have any burdens—only my youngest brother. Do you mean You'll heal him from his insanity and he can make his own living?"

That evening in prayer meeting she had a burden for the brother and requested prayer for him. She looked at the clock—it was 8:10. Her heart was at peace—she would ask forgiveness of him for Monday's hot words.

It was 10 p.m. when she reached home. The brother was still out. An alarm sounded in her mind and just minutes later police were at the door. "Is W your relative?"

"Yes, that is my brother. What is wrong?"

"He just jumped off the sixth floor of a shopping mall and he is dead." For the next two hours they questioned her until they were satisfied that it was really a suicide and no foul play. His previous failed attempts, his threats that next time he would jump from a higher level and his complaints that the doctor's medicine dried his mouth were confirmation of intention. According to the security guard who found his body, he had jumped between 8:00 and 8:15 p.m. while L was in prayer meeting.

L cried inconsolably all day and all night blaming his death on herself. If only she had not gotten angry with him. It was five weeks to the day since his sister-in-law's death. This was the third family funeral in the nine months since L's mother died. How much sorrow could one heart bear? L gathered her brother's best jeans, jacket and dark glasses to dress his body. It made him look peaceful as though he were going out for an evening with his friends. At age 31 he was released from his earthly problems. In such a case we could only rest in God's mercy. Before his mind was scrambled by drugs, the man had made a profession of faith and had been baptized. What he did in a time of unbalanced mind was for God to judge.

Again the cell group rallied to support the mourners. It was like a repetitious nightmare as the family blamed one another in their pain and sorrow. None of the brothers and sisters had ever helped W in life except L. She had shouldered all his needs. But they blamed her Christianity for all the bad luck. We mingled once again with the grieving family; they warmed up quickly.

We were 50 Christians and they were only a dozen non-Christians who sadly gathered at the Buddhist temple pavilion that day. I sat on the floor with the family members who were folding fake paper money to put in a paper suitcase beside a paper house. It was a Chinese custom to provide for the needs of the deceased in the next world.

A partially intoxicated brother apologetically explained to me, "We don't know if he gets it or if it helps. We do it as tradition." I assured him he could do whatever relieved his sorrow. I was there to be a friend in time of need.

A lone wreath (from our church members) was propped against the casket. Apart from the family, only two friends came. They had heard of the suicide on TV Wednesday night and recognized his name. A perfunctory Buddhist chant was given by three monks. We Christians simply sat respectfully with our hands in our laps, rather than in the Buddhist worship posture. When the monks finished, they filed out to another pavilion for their next appointment.

Our pastor then got up and preached and we sang a couple of songs. We were a little ill at ease doing this for the first time in a temple pavilion. True, I had experienced a similar situation at Auntie Pong's death up in Sisaket, but this was Bangkok city. Here the family had requested both a Buddhist and a Christian ceremony and the head abbot had granted permission. Refreshments were served and then the family took the paper money and items out to burn them to heaven.

A guest at another pavilion wandered over to us. He quizzically asked, "Is there a priest here? Or a Catholic father?"

"No. We have our preacher pastor here."

"You mean Christians can come to the temple?" he asked incredulously.

"Oh, yes, we come to be a comfort to the living." We launched into a Gospel witness and shared some tracts with him. Singing Christian songs in a Buddhist temple was not the usual order of the day and had caught the attention of this man.

On the day of cremation the family members—men in particular--may be drunk and crying loudly. It was so with L's next oldest brother. As the body began to burn he wailed, "I've been to many cremations, but this time it is my brother they are burning!" Our hearts ached deeply with this poor sorrowing family.

A brother-in-law opened a conversation with me. "I'm really impressed with Pastor T. He preaches clearly. You people are so friendly and almost like family with us. You greet us and help us like you are one of us—but then all the religions lead to the same place." I praised the Lord. There was a crack in his hard heart and God's love was seeping into it!

It was not God's plan that L should be aborted. The one whose life her mother had tried to end was the very one who was the means of the mother finding life without end! That life shone brightly in spite of mistakes and flaws. Her burden lifted, L could now pursue God's leading in seminary. She called me aside one day, "What did you say to the church team about me?"

"What do you mean?" I asked.

"Why are they giving me full tuition to seminary?" she asked.

"I had nothing to do with it! I learned about it from a deacon," I replied.

"Oh, wow," she said. "That confirms God's leading. He is providing."

Home in California on my sixth home assignment I received a letter from L. It was an update of her family news and her seminary studies. The letter ended: "Sunday was Mother's Day. My mother is in heaven, but you are my spiritual mother." Enclosed was a rather smashed artificial jasmine flower—a memento from the church's outreach on Mother's Day. Tears came to my eyes.

184

Returning home for my sixth home assignment I was presented with a new challenge. My parents had moved from their large home of 40 years to a new town, Chino Hills, California, population 58,000. In seeking for a place to live, my last choice for an apartment was God's first choice. I took the only available apartment—an upstairs studio. The credit union was shocked by my low missionary allowance and was on the verge of denying me the rental. "This is your salary per week—er, is it two weeks?" the girl asked hesitantly.

"No, it's a monthly allowance," I answered. "I get along fine. I travel to churches and they take care of me. It's enough." It took a notarized guarantee of rental payment from the national office in Colorado Springs to persuade them I was a good risk renter!

I soon found this apartment actually had more floor space than my one bedroom unit of last home assignment. My fear of noisy teenagers with boom boxes all night in these family apartments was unfounded. To my delight, the mornings were quiet and the swimming pool outside my window was unoccupied until afternoons. God had blessed me abundantly. He knew better than I what I needed in order to write it all down. This was the year I needed to write my autobiography.

As a child I had learned to speak "Siamese." That same language was called "Thai" by the time I was preparing to be a missionary. When I was a child the missionaries served five year terms in Thailand followed by a 12-14 month "furlough." Travel to and from the homeland was cheapest by slow freighter ships. By the time I went out to the mission field as a missionary myself, the cheaper mode of travel was by plane. Our terms of service were shortened to four year spans. The hiatus between them eventually was called a home assignment.

Some things however do not change. God still keeps His promises and people are still in need of a Savior. My own call to be a missionary in 1957 and my call to intercession 23 years later have never been rescinded either.

My journal entry for September 3, 1999 was a prayer:

Lord, I've never sought riches but yet You've given me riches! A rich heritage of a godly family who are rich in love for You and love for me.

I'm rich with experiences and adventures on four continents and over 20 countries because You called my parents and then me to serve You overseas.

I'm rich in friendships and acquaintances You've brought across my paths--men, women and children of all ages and diverse nationalities.

Thank you for the riches of Your Word in my heart and mind—not in just one language, but two!

I'm rich in health—I have all my body parts—both arms and both legs, my own teeth and adequate hair—and everything works!

Thank you, Lord, You've showered me with so much to give. The state may label me as "low income" because they narrowly focus on pennies and nickels and dimes. But real riches are priceless...I have great joy and happiness; peace that transcends the circumstances around me; job satisfaction independent of bosses, co-workers, workplace or hours; abounding hope and challenges that know no limits. You've enriched me with humor and ideas in just the right mix to bring glory to Yourself—THE ULTIMATE in richness.

Thank you for Your graciousness, Oh, Lord. Please help me to be a worthy steward of all You have entrusted to me!

At the age of five I had put my trust in Jesus as my Savior. At seven I had experienced His saving hand on my physical life when I was shot in the leg with a stud on shipboard returning to Thailand. Repeatedly as a child and later as a missionary I was healed of a heart condition, sinus headaches, sunstroke, emotional overload and multiple minor illnesses. God healed my memories of a traumatic robbery.

I found I could trust God to guide me to the right college and saw Him open doors to nursing and midwifery training on His time schedule. He provided Christian friends for my social needs. As He clothed the lilies of the field so He surprised me with a darling white summer suit and winter apparel when needed. On two sides of the ocean God proved to be my car mechanic. No less adept was He in the kitchen—coconut custard was the proof.

God called me to be a missionary, a nurse, an intercessor. In each call He stayed alongside as my Enabler. Although fulfilling His call led me through countless dangers on highways or in cities, His angels were on duty to protect me. In a tornado, at a broken bridge or on a harrowing bus ride He was there. He continuously directed not only my physical path, but also my spiritual journey. He led me to a network of hungry souls--from a doctor's clinic in a small town in northeast Thailand to the nameless masses of Bangkok's millions. God took me out of my comfort zone to befriend western Buddhist nuns and monks and a Thai governor. He proved that His Word would produce fruit whether sowed 50 years ago by my parents as pioneer missionaries in a dusty little Thai town, or as a gospel tract in the outskirts of Bangkok.

God released me from an assortment of fears, then gifted me for each task He brought my way—knowledge to care for a leprosy patient and wisdom as MK school nurse. Whether teaching TEE to barely literate village Christians or mentoring young college graduates in the metropolis of Bangkok, God gave the flexibility.

The seasons of tears were all but forgotten by the abundant joy of seeing God at work all around. He overwhelmingly proved His Word. Proverbs 3:5-6 *"Trust* in the LORD with *all* your heart (even for the mosquitoes of the past) and lean *not* on your own understanding (God, this computer challenged lady needs Your help!); in *all* your ways acknowledge him, and *he* will make your paths straight (for the days and years ahead)." [Emphasis and parenthesis mine.]

What was it that kept me on the mission field for 35 years? I think I know the answer. It was God proving His Word to be true again and again. It was the godly heritage I was given and the faithful prayer partners, who brought it all to pass. In the recounting of His works has come a recurrent blessing!

As I had said at my 48th birthday celebration, "Whatever you see in me that is commendable or lovable is really Jesus. He lives within me. He chose what family I should be born into and where I would live."

THANK YOU, LORD.

THANK YOU, PRAYER PARTNERS.

Harvey and Grace Boese with infant Joy to Siam December, 1946

Graduate Nurse
Los Angeles County
General Hospital
School of Nursing
1967

Joy with siblings: Faith, Timothy, Carol and Melody
1966

Joy harvesting rice in Maranatha
1975

Wearing a Thai wrap around
skirt Joy teaches in a church
1976

Nurse Joy with leprosy patients at Maranatha Clinic, Khonkaen
1975

Joy had an elephant ride enroute to church. She climbed from the porch into a basket on the elephant's back.
1977

The leprosy Christian who wanted to study TEE paid for his book with a bushel of garlic.
1977

The Chaiyapoom Church—one of the WMPF Portable Chapel Projects
1982

The governor and his wife in formal dress
1983

The day Usha left the temple Joy and Thai Christians
pose with Usha and Kirsten (still in nuns' robes).
1980

Auntie S the fortune teller friend in
Sisaket who liked to study the Bible
1989

Miss D (Joy's forever friend)
1990

Mrs. SJ's young son Pongsuk (directly behind her) saw God
answer prayer with a bowl of noodles.
1986

L and her mother who accepted
Christ in 1998

Harvey and Grace Boese (aged 82
and 78) visiting Joy in Bangkok
January 1999

Mrs. Somsee, daughter and two grandchildren
2000

Boese sibling reunion January, 2004 in California
Joy, Faith, Tim, Carol, Melody

Harvey and Grace Boese
December 2004